NUTRITION & HEALTH

Junk Food Junkies

CARLA MOONEY

LUCENT BOOKS
A part of Gale, Cengage Learning

GALE
CENGAGE Learning

Detroit • New York • San Francisco • New Haven, Conn • Waterville, Maine • London

LIBRARY OF CONGRESS CATALOGING-IN-PUBLICATION DATA

Mooney, Carla, 1970-
  Junk food junkies / by Carla Mooney.
    p. cm. -- (Nutrition and health)
  Includes bibliographical references and index.
  ISBN 978-1-4205-0271-8 (hardcover)
  1. Junk food--Health aspects. I. Title.
  TX370.M66 2010
  641.5'638--dc22

                                                    2010016858

Lucent Books
27500 Drake Rd.
Farmington Hills, MI 48331

ISBN-13: 978-1-4205-0271-8
ISBN-10: 1-4205-0271-9

Printed in the United States of America
3 4 5 6 7 14 13 12 11

TABLE OF CONTENTS

FOREWORD

Many people today are often amazed by the amount of nutrition and health information, often contradictory, that can be found in the media. Television, newspapers, and magazines bombard readers with the latest news and recommendations. Television news programs report on recent scientific studies. The healthy living sections of newspapers and magazines offer information and advice. In addition, electronic media such as Web sites, blogs, and forums post daily nutrition and health news and recommendations.

This constant stream of information can be confusing. The science behind nutrition and health is constantly evolving. Current research often leads to new ideas and insights. Many times, the latest nutrition studies and health recommendations contradict previous studies or traditional health advice. When the media report these changes without giving context or explanations, consumers become confused. In a survey by the National Health Council, for example, 68 percent of participants agreed that "when reporting medical and health news, the media often contradict themselves, so I don't know what to believe." In addition, the Food Marketing Institute reported that eight out of ten consumers thought it was likely that nutrition and health experts would have a completely different idea about what foods are healthy within five years. With so much contradictory information, people have difficulty deciding how to apply nutrition and health recommendations to their lives. Students find it difficult to find relevant yet clear and credible information for reports.

Changing recommendations for antioxidant supplements are an example of how confusion can arise. In the 1990s antioxidants, such as vitamins C and E and beta-carotene, came to the public's attention. Scientists found that people who ate more antioxidant-rich foods had a lower risk of heart disease, cancer, vision loss, and other chronic conditions than those who ate lower amounts. Without waiting for more scientific study, the media and supplement companies quickly spread the word that antioxidants could help fight and prevent disease. They recommended that people take antioxidant supplements and eat fortified foods. When further scientific studies were completed, however, most did not support the initial recommendations. While naturally occurring antioxidants in fruits and vegetables may help prevent a variety of chronic diseases, little scientific evidence proved antioxidant supplements had the same effect. In fact, a study published in the November 2008 *Journal of the American Medical Association* found that supplemental vitamins A and C gave no more heart protection than a placebo. The study's results contradicted the widely publicized recommendation, leading to consumer confusion. This example highlights the importance of context for evaluating nutrition and health news. Understanding a topic's scientific background, interpreting a study's findings, and evaluating news sources are critical skills that help reduce confusion.

Lucent's Nutrition and Health series is designed to help young people sift through the mountain of confusing facts, opinions, and recommendations. Each book contains the most up-to-date information, synthesized and written so that students can understand and think critically about nutrition and health issues. Each volume of the series provides a balanced overview of today's hot-button nutrition and health issues while presenting the latest scientific findings and a discussion of issues surrounding the topic. The series provides young people with tools for evaluating conflicting and ever-changing ideas about nutrition and health. Clear narrative peppered with personal anecdotes, fully documented primary and secondary source quotes, informative sidebars, fact boxes, and statistics are all used to help readers understand these topics and how they affect their bodies and their lives. Each volume includes information about changes in trends over time, political controversies, and international perspectives. Full-color photographs and charts enhance all volumes in the series. The Nutrition and Health series is a valuable resource for young people to understand current topics and make informed choices for themselves.

Junk Food Society

L ess than a century ago most people cooked fresh foods at home. They rarely ate in restaurants. If they did, the restaurant chefs also cooked fresh, home-style meals. A convenient snack was a handful of fresh fruit or vegetables.

In the last few decades, however, the eating habits of Americans and people around the world have changed dramatically. Meals and snacks are quick, fast, and processed. Today people indulge daily in easy-to-eat candy, chips, hot dogs, and french fries. They eat doughnuts for breakfast, fast food hamburgers for lunch, and pizza for dinner. In 1972 Michael Jacobson, cofounder of the Center for Science in the Public Interest, gave these types of food a name. He called them "junk foods" because they provided little nutrition and were loaded with calories and harmful fats.

Since that time, the popularity of junk food has skyrocketed. Today it is a part of American society and culture. Junk food is also quickly spreading around the world. Part of the reason junk food is so popular is that it is convenient and cheap to buy. Many families no longer have a parent who waits for the kids to come home from school and prepares meals. Instead, two parents work, or a single parent heads the household. After a long day at the office, many busy families find it easier to heat a frozen dinner in the microwave or pick up a hamburger at the fast food drive-through.

This shift toward junk food, however, is linked to numerous health problems. Junk food is rich in calories but low in nutrition. Most junk food contains little protein, vitamins, or minerals found in fresh foods such as lean meats, low-fat dairy products, fruits, and vegetables. Instead, junk food contains large quantities of fats and sugars. Although the body needs moderate amounts of fat and sugar to work properly, large quantities can be harmful. Eating junk food in excess can have short-term and longer-term effects on a person's health. In the short term junk food can make a person feel sluggish. He or she might have a harder time concentrating. After a big, fatty meal, a person might feel nauseated. Over a longer period the health effects of junk food become more serious. A diet rich in junk food has been linked to several serious conditions and diseases such as obesity, heart disease, and cancer.

After a long day, many families find it easier to heat a frozen dinner than prepare a whole nutritious meal.

Obesity, in particular, has become a national epidemic. Americans are fatter now than at any other time in history. Millions of children, teens, and adults carry around extra pounds. They suffer emotionally and physically from the extra weight. Obesity-related conditions, such as type 2 diabetes, are on the rise.

These trends alarm many concerned parents and health experts. As a result, arguments over junk food have broken out in homes, schools, and communities. Some believe that eating junk food is a personal choice. Others argue that junk food is as unhealthy and addictive as tobacco and alcohol. Some people want schools to ban junk food. Some are even calling for the government to regulate and restrict junk food.

For certain people junk food has no place in a healthy diet. Others believe that junk foods can be enjoyed in moderation as part of a healthy diet. Regardless, understanding the basics of nutrition can help people make informed choices about eating junk food. Many people believe that education about nutrition should start at a young age. "We feel we have such an opportunity . . . to teach children not only what they need to be eating, but why they need to be eating this way," said Janey Thornton, president of the School Nutrition Association. "That's something they can use every day for the rest of their lives."[1]

CHAPTER 1

The Popularity of Junk Food

On a typical weekday thirteen-year-old Sophie Martin immediately heads for the kitchen pantry when she gets home from school. She grabs a bag of cheese curls and tosses them two at a time into her mouth. Next, she searches through the shelves for chocolate—M&M's, Oreos, Hershey's Kisses. A few hours later she eats dinner with her family. Grilled pork, yellow corn, and green salad sit practically untouched on her plate. Before long she pushes away from the table. "I'm full," she claims. Fifteen minutes later Sophie rummages through the pantry again. This time she looks for the jumbo chocolate chip cookies her mom bought earlier in the day. Finding them, she grabs one and blissfully sinks her teeth into the gooey chocolate.

What Is Junk Food?

The human body needs food to fuel its activity. Nutrients such as protein, vitamins, and minerals enable the body to grow, move, and function well. Foods such as fresh fruit, vegetables, lean meats, low-fat dairy, and grains are full of nutrients that efficiently fuel the body. They also contain the small amount of sugar and fat that the body needs. The average teen needs no more than 25 to 35 percent of his or her daily calories from fat and 10 percent from sugar in his or her diet.

Like Sophie, however, many people fill their bodies with junk food instead of nutrient-rich foods. Junk food is any type of food that has unhealthy amounts of salt, sugar, or fat in it. The large amount of sugar and fat usually makes junk food high in calories. It has few nutrients, which is why some people say that junk food has empty calories. Salty chips, candy, gum, cookies, cakes, ice cream, fried fast food, and soda are some of the major types of junk food. Some foods become unhealthy by the way they are prepared—for example, chicken fried into crispy tenders or popcorn cooked in oil and drenched in butter.

The Rise in Junk Food

Sophie is not the only one reaching for a cookie. According to a 2004 study, 25 percent of the food eaten by Americans is nutrient-poor junk food. Kids are more likely to reach for a soda or fruit punch than milk or orange juice. Teens will grab a bag of potato chips or candy bar instead of cutting up raw vegetables for a snack. In fact, for many people the only "vegetable" that crosses their lips on a regular basis is french fries. "Junk food is ever present and inexpensive. Society today enjoys immediate gratification. So if any person—not even just a teen—has a dollar in their pocket and sees a package of chips in front of them, they're likely to indulge,"[2] says Laurie Beebe, a registered dietician who specializes in weight-loss management.

The trend toward eating junk food is a recent phenomenon. For thousands of years humans showed a remarkable ability to determine just the right amount of fuel their bodies needed. Meals were prepared at home and slow-cooked with fresh, nutritious ingredients. "A hundred years ago snack food did not exist—nothing you could pop open and over-eat," says Mollie Katzen, author of *The Moosewood Cookbook* and a consultant to Harvard Dining Services. "There were

A nineteenth-century woman stirs a cooking pot. There was no junk food during this era since foods took a long time to be prepared.

stew pots. Things took a long time to cook, and a meal was the result of someone's labor."[3]

In addition, most adults ate only the amount of food they needed. Weight stayed relatively stable, neither rising nor falling by significant amounts. Those who ate too much and became overweight were the exception rather than the rule.

In the second half of the twentieth century, however, things began to change. Katherine Flegal, a senior research scientist at the Centers for Disease Control and Prevention, noticed an unusual trend. While she was studying data on the health and nutritional status of Americans, she saw a dramatic increase in the number of overweight and obese people. In 1960 the average body mass index for men and women was about 25; by 2002 the average body mass index had increased to almost 28 for men and just over 28 for women. Americans were getting fatter at an alarming rate. In addition, many people were gaining the weight as children and teens.

NUTRITION FACT

One 12-oz. (340g) can of Coke

Contains 145 calories and 40.5 grams of sugar

Researchers wondered what was behind this disturbing trend. The math of weight gain is simple. If a person eats more calories than the body needs, the excess calories are stored as fat. Flegal looked to see what had changed to make Americans weigh more. One trend she noticed was a change in Americans' eating habits.

Since the 1970s the culture of eating has shifted in America. Rather than sitting down for a home-cooked meal, more people eat out or grab a quick bite to go. Fast food and chain restaurants have exploded across the country. Today nearly every town has a McDonald's or a Burger King. Martinsburg, West Virginia, is like many towns around the nation. In 1970 Martinsburg had six fast food restaurants; by 2006 it had more than forty. Processed junk foods also fill grocery store shelves. These foods are easy to buy and ready to eat. Much of the fast food and processed foods are also loaded with fat, sugar, and salt. More and more people are eating this junk food.

Anatomy of MyPyramid

In 2005, the U.S. Department of Agriculture released this new food pyramid. It is designed to help Americans take a personalized approach to diet and lifestyle. It shows the recommended proportion of foods from each food group. Physical activity is a new addition to the pyramid.

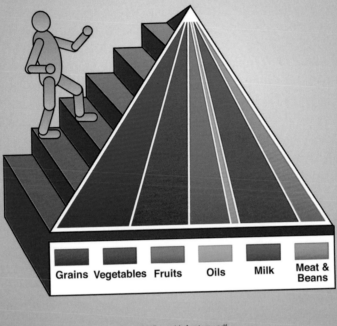

Grains Vegetables Fruits Oils Milk Meat & Beans

Taken from: www.mypyramid.gov/downloads/MyPyramid_Anatomy.pdf.

What people drink has also changed. Soda has exploded in popularity across all age groups. A recent study in California found that around 41 percent of children, 62 percent of adolescents, and 24 percent of adults consume one or more sodas per day. The average California teen consumes 39 pounds of sugar a year from soda alone.

Convenient and Cheap

One reason junk food is so popular is that it is an easy choice. According to a Pew Research study, 73 percent of people said they eat junk food because it is convenient. Junk

Fast Food Around the World

Cui Tao, a twenty-four-year-old in Tianjin, China, wanted to take his girlfriend to a special restaurant on Valentine's Day. They had to wait an hour for a table. The meal cost more than one-fourth of his monthly income. Tao says that their dinner at Pizza Hut was worth it. He added that the couple dines at Pizza Hut about twelve times a year.

Tao's experience at Pizza Hut is one example of how the overseas market for fast food is booming. In 1991 McDonald's had fewer than four thousand restaurants outside the United States. By the end of 2008, the company had exploded to almost thirty-two thousand restaurants in 118 countries. McDonald's has restaurants in Russia, Egypt, and Argentina. Other fast food restaurants have followed the move overseas, including Burger King, Pizza Hut, and Kentucky Fried Chicken (KFC). In June 2008, Pizza Hut added fifty new locations, bringing its international total to more than five hundred restaurants.

Soda companies, such as PepsiCo and Coca-Cola, are also expanding sales overseas. In Latin America Coca-Cola's partner, Panamaco, started a marketing program called the 100 Meters Program. The companies want to sell Coke in supermarkets, schools, office buildings, and newsstands. They have even hired vendors to sell Coke at traffic lights in Venezuela. "The objective of this program is simple. In any urban center no one should have to walk more than 100 meters to buy our products," said Panamaco.

Eric Schlosser and Charles Wilson, *Chew on This: Everything You Don't Want to Know About Fast Food.* Boston: Houghton Mifflin, 2006, p. 237.

A McDonald's in Moscow, Russia.

food eliminates most preparing or cooking of food. Chips and cookies can be eaten right out of the bag. Fast food restaurants serve entire meals in minutes. Even at home, frozen dinners can be popped in the microwave and cooked quickly. "When I'm shuttling the kids to gymnastics, soccer, and karate after school, sometimes it's a lot easier to stop at McDonald's than to cook dinner,"[4] says Ellen Martin, Sophie's mother.

Junk food is also cheap. According to the Pew Research study, 24 percent of people said that they choose junk food because it is more affordable than healthy food. At the grocery store a bag of frozen chicken nuggets at $3.33 per pound costs less than a package of fresh chicken breasts at $4.99 a pound. Fast food meals cost much less than healthier restaurant dinners. A fast food hamburger, fries, and soda costs around five dollars, while just an entree salad at a restaurant averages nine dollars. For those on a tight budget, cost matters.

Tempting Ads

The junk food industry spends billions of dollars each year to market their products. Ads for fast food restaurants dominate television, magazines, and billboards. They often feature young, fit people enjoying junk food. Some companies pay famous celebrities and athletes to advertise their products. Television shows, especially for kids, are full of commercials for cookies, sugared cereals, fruit snacks, and candy.

A billboard advertises Ponderosa's all-you-can-eat buffet. The food industry spends billions each year to market its products.

In many cases, advertising can be a powerful influence on buyers. With the constant ads and reminders, a burger for lunch starts to sound like a good idea. When shopping at the store, the memory of catchy commercials often prompts kids and parents to put a bag of cookies into the grocery cart.

It Tastes Good

Convenience and price might get people to try junk food, but taste is what keeps them coming back for more. "Junk food companies have figured out that humans are driven by the taste and experience of foods that are high in fat, sugar and sodium. They sugarcoat and fry foods repeatedly to get the ingredients that stimulate us to consume these foods repeatedly,"[5] says dietitian Laurie Beebe. Most people like the taste of sweet and salty foods. Junk food uses combinations of oils, fats, sugars, and salt to make food more flavorful.

Scientists describe certain foods, such as many junk foods, as palatable. "Palatable foods arouse our appetite. They act as an incentive to eat,"[6] said Peter Rogers, a biological psychologist at the University of Bristol in England.

For years researchers have known that people prefer sugar in their food. Newborns given a mixture of sugar and water show pleasure in their facial expressions. Sugar alone, however, is not enough to make a food taste good. Researchers have found that the most palatable foods have some combination of sugar, fat, and salt, such as creamy milkshakes or crunchy french fries dipped in sweetened ketchup. Fat "is responsible for the characteristic texture, flavor and aroma of many foods and largely determines the palatability of the diet,"[7] said researcher Adam Drewnowski of the University of Washington in Seattle.

Researchers believe that humans may have a taste receptor for fats. In a study at the University of Bourgogne in France, scientists found a receptor protein on mouse tongues

NUTRITION FACT

28% and 20%

Percentage of women and men, respectively, in the United States that eat at least five servings of fruits and vegetables per day that makes fats tasty to the animals. They believe humans may have the same taste receptor. That may explain why adding creamy dressings to salads or butter to baked potatoes makes them taste so good. "There is a clear evolutionary advantage to having a taste bud for lipids [fats]," said Nada Abumrad, a nutritional researcher at Washington University School of Medicine in St Louis. "It showed our ancestors that fatty foods are good for us because they allow us to store energy."[8] Early humans did not shop at a store for their food. Instead, they had to hunt, gather, or grow anything they ate. Having stored fats or energy allowed humans to survive during times when food was not readily available.

The Right Mix

Fat alone is not enough to tempt a person to eat more. When fat is combined with sugar and salt, however, the mix can become irresistible. The perfect combination of fats, sugars, and salt is different for everyone. That is why one person might be tempted by a double chocolate ice cream cone, while another cannot pass up a heaping plate of cheesy nachos. When the mix is right, however, it acts

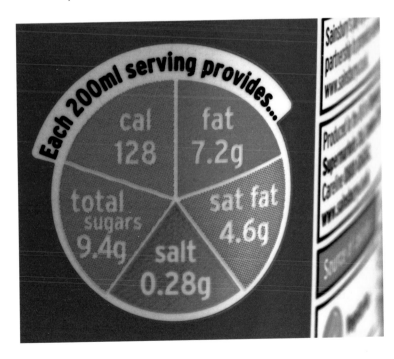

When the mix of sugars, fats, and salt is right it can be a powerful pull to eat more.

Immigrants Struggle with Junk Food

Thirteen-year-old Adrian McHargh was active and fit in his hometown of Kingston, Jamaica. He swam in the ocean and ate the healthy dinners his mother cooked. When his family moved to America, however, Adrian's eating habits changed. New fast foods and packaged foods were inexpensive and tasty. Adrian loved toaster waffles, corn dogs, and chocolate syrup. He also spent more time indoors, watching television. Within months Adrian's new lifestyle caught up with him. He had gained 30 pounds (13.6kg). He also had hypertension and high cholesterol and was at an increased risk of developing type 2 diabetes.

Pat Crawford is the codirector of the Center for Weight and Health at the University of California–Berkeley. He says that many immigrants fall into the same trap as Adrian and overindulge on American junk food. "We really would like to encourage immigrant families to continue the kinds of eating that they ate in their country of origin because our studies show that the longer they've been in this country the more likely that their children are going to get fat,"[1] says Crawford.

Since receiving a warning from doctors, Adrian has reduced junk food eating and has been exercising more. He has lost weight, and his cholesterol levels are normal again. "I'm buying more eggs and more yogurt," says his mother. "More organic foods—organic peanut butter. I'm doing a lot of vegetables—fresh vegetables. Carrots. Potatoes. Broccoli."[2]

1. Quoted in John Bonifield, "Immigrant Children Struggle with America's Junk Food," CNN. www.cnn.com/2007/ HEALTH/diet.fitness/09/05/kd.adrians.story.

2. Quoted in Bonifield, "Immigrant Children Struggle with America's Junk Food."

as a powerful incentive to eat more. Barry Levin, a professor at the New Jersey Medical School, demonstrated this incentive in an experiment with two groups of rats. The first group always overfed when a high-calorie diet was made available to them. When given the same food, the second group did not overfeed and reduced eating after taking in extra calories. When Levin gave both groups a rich, creamy liquid high in sugar and fat, their eating patterns changed. All of the rats ate without restraint. "They will just gorge themselves,"[9] said Levin. A high-fat diet alone did not prompt the rats to overeat and become fat. The right combination of sugar and fat did.

Ultra-Processed and Flavored

Companies refine and process junk food so that it is easy and pleasurable to eat. They also process foods to reduce spoilage and increase a food's shelf life. Processing removes items in whole foods like fiber and gristle that are harder to chew. The resulting food is easy to eat and swallow. In the past Americans chewed each mouthful about twenty-five times before they swallowed. Now the average mouthful of processed food is chewed only ten times. "These refined versions of salt, fat, sugar and grains are literally irresistible. Mounds of it go down quickly and easily and kids are not full. Again, it's no accident; how much texture is in the bun of fast food burgers or a package of Ho-Ho's?"[10] said Nancy Jerominski, a fitness and health consultant.

All that processing also destroys a food's natural flavor. So the flavor industry steps in to make processed food taste good. International Flavors and Fragrances is one of the world's largest flavor companies. They mix and match hundreds of flavor chemicals to find just the right taste. The company's snack-and-savory lab creates flavors for potato chips, corn chips, breads, crackers, and breakfast cereals. The confectionery lab works on flavors for ice cream, cookies, and candies. The beverage lab devises flavors for soft drinks, sports drinks, bottled teas, and other beverages. The flavor chemicals add taste to junk food but do not add any nutrients.

Physical Reaction

Not only does junk food taste good, it can become addictive. Like many teens, thirteen-year-old Morgan thinks about chocolate a lot and often craves it. "I like chocolate; it's soft and tastes good. It's in a lot of different foods," she says. "I want a variety of different chocolates."[11] A craving often happens at the same time of day. It can be specific, so that not just any food will satisfy; only the right combination of sugar and fat will do.

For years researchers believed that food cravings occurred when the body needed certain nutrients. For example, if the body were low on salt, people would crave salty foods to compensate. This theory does not explain why people crave salty foods even when they are not salt deficient. Instead, new research has turned to the brain's pleasure center.

The brain's pleasure center guides a person to behaviors that help ensure survival, such as eating, reproducing, exercising, and interacting with others. When an experience gives pleasure, the brain releases endorphins such as dopamine. These feel-good chemicals lock onto brain cells and build a memory of the pleasure.

Tasty junk food that is high in fat and sugar produces a strong reaction in the brain's pleasure center. In fact, the reaction to junk food is similar to the reward effect of drugs like morphine and heroin. Neal Barnard, founder of the Physicians Committee for Responsible Medicine, agrees that the combination of sugar and fat can make junk food addictive. "It's not that you lack willpower," he says. "These

When an experience gives pleasure, the brain releases endorphins like dopamine. Tasty junk food that is high in fat and sugar can cause a similar effect in the brain.

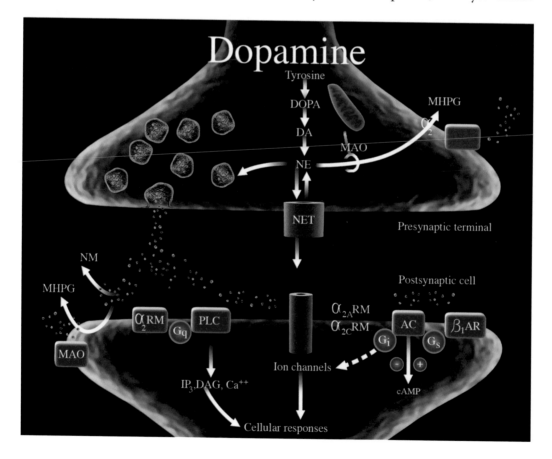

foods stimulate the release of chemicals in the brain's pleasure center that keep you hooked."[12]

Eating junk food can quickly become a hard habit to break. In one study researchers gave people a high-sugar, high-fat snack at the same time for five consecutive days. For several days after the test, the people found they craved something sweet at about the same time each day that they had eaten the study snack. Before the study the people had never snacked at that time. It had taken only five days to establish the junk food habit.

Comfort Food

Although junk food has little nutritional value, it might help people cope in times of trouble. When stressed, some people find themselves gorging on chocolate or cookies. Others dive into chips or fried food. The junk food industry encourages this behavior. Ads show their products as a reward for a tough day and a relaxing way to self-indulge.

According to physiologist Mary Dallman at the University of California–San Francisco, people may eat junk food in times of stress for physical reasons. She says that fat and sugar lower stress hormones and calm the brain. "That's why we call them comfort foods,"[13] she said.

Professor Margaret Morris from the University of New South Wales in Australia reported similar findings in studies with rats. During the experiments, the researchers separated baby rats from their mothers. Some ate food high in fat and sugar. The others ate a healthy diet. The researchers found that the rats that ate food high in fat and sugar showed less stress and agitation. "The same reaction is likely to occur in humans because the brain pathways that regulate appetite in rats are similar to those in humans,"[14] said Morris.

One Is Not Enough

Not only can junk food be tempting and addictive, it may also cause a person to eat more. "My grandmother always has this jar of Hershey Kisses. I'd take one and then I tell myself that I'm just going to have one, it will be OK. The

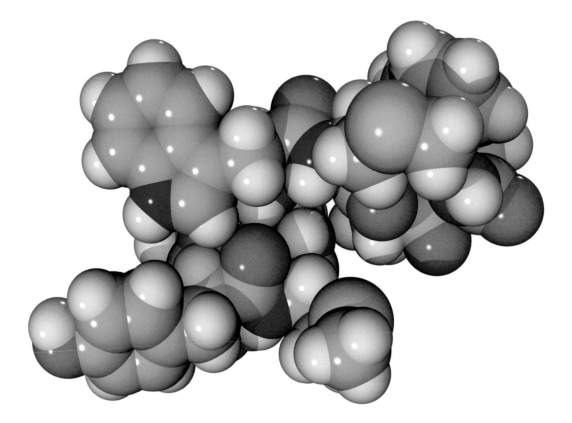

next thing I know I've taken all of them,"[15] says thirteen-year-old Morgan. Like Morgan, many people have trouble limiting junk food once they start eating. Because many children and teens have less impulse control than adults, they can have an even harder time controlling a junk food impulse.

New research shows that foods high in fat may suppress a hormone in the brain that tells the body when it is full. Normally, this hormone, called cholecystokinin (CCK), signals the body to stop eating. A 2005 study at the Neuroscience Institute at Penn State University tracked two groups of rats, one fed a high-fat diet and the other fed a low-fat diet. When researchers injected both groups of rats with CCK, the rats eating low-fat food stopped or lessened their eating. The second group, however, kept enjoying their high-fat foods without any signs of stopping. The CCK had no effect on them. The results may explain why many people find it so hard to eat just one cookie or chip.

Genetic Factors

Some researchers believe that genes might play a role in whether a person eats junk food. In the *New England Journal of Medicine*, British researchers report that children with a certain gene are more likely to eat energy-dense foods such as high calorie junk food. "What [this study] effectively shows is that people with the relevant variants on the gene have a trait which may lead them to eat more unhealthy, fattening foods,"[16] said study senior author Colin Palmer, chair of pharmacogenomics in the Biomedical Research Institute at the University of Dundee. The finding may explain why some people are more attracted to junk food. The scientists stress, however, that having the gene does not mean a person is destined to gorge on junk food.

Junk food has become a daily part of many people's lives. Whether it is chips, cookies, or soda, people are eating and drinking junk food at a tremendous rate. The irresistible pull of all that fat and sugar keeps them coming back for more.

CHAPTER 2

How Junk Food Affects Your Health

Junk food may taste good, but eating too much can have serious effects on the body. Too much junk food can make a person feel bloated, lethargic, or sick. Even worse, the enormous amounts of fat, sugar, and salt in junk food can contribute to several serious and sometimes fatal diseases.

Slowing Down and Feeling Sick

"Whenever I eat junk food, I feel as if my whole routine has slowed down . . . all I want to do is sleep,"[17] says seventeen-year-old Caiti. Her experience is common. After people eat, their bodies convert carbohydrates into a sugar called glucose, or blood sugar. The glucose then enters the bloodstream. Carbohydrates provide fuel for the body's muscles and brain. Not all carbohydrates are digested at the same rate. Some carbohydrates, such as those found in whole-grain bread and apples, are digested slowly and produce a gradual rise in blood sugar. These are called complex carbohydrates. Other carbohydrates, called simple, are rapidly digested and absorbed into the body. These carbohydrates can make blood sugar levels spike quickly and have a high glycemic index value. The glycemic index ranks carbohydrates according to how they affect blood sugar. Food like potatoes and white bread have a high glycemic index. They cause large fluctuations in blood sugar levels. After eating these foods, a person may have a short burst of energy and an improved mood. Many junk foods, such as jellybeans, doughnuts, and corn chips, also have a high glycemic index.

The blood sugar spike from eating such foods does not last long. Blood sugar levels drop again, sometimes below the starting level. The dramatic fall is called a "crash." During a crash a person may feel sleepy and less active. Some people

Because of their high glycemic index, foods like doughnuts, jelly beans, and chips can cause a person to have a short burst of energy.

also feel shaky and irritable. These symptoms occur because the drop in blood sugar triggers the body's hormone defense mechanism. The body releases or reduces certain hormones such as glucagon to raise blood sugar levels. Nancy Jerominski, a nutrition and fitness consultant, often talks to high school students about the pitfalls of junk food. At one school she issued a challenge to students:

> The majority of these kids were at least 30 pounds overweight, had bad skin and were literally dragging their backsides into class in the morning. They were lethargic and listless. Most had eaten no breakfast or were drinking what I call "crack in a can" (Red Bull type energy drinks), soda or coffee. If they did eat breakfast, they'd stopped at McDonald's, had a donut or boxed cereal. After lunch, this same sleepy bunch was nearly uncontrollable and then they all crashed about an hour later. I challenged them to just cut back on their intake of sugar and junk food.[18]

Several weeks later Jerominski returned to the school. She found that the students who had taken her challenge saw a marked improvement in how they felt. "Every single one of [them] told me they felt better, they had more energy and they slept better,"[19] she says.

Sometimes eating too much junk food can make a person feel sick. Fifteen-year-old Jack typically filled his plate with healthy food at home. When out with friends, however, he found it harder to make healthy choices. When his friend wanted to stop at a fast food restaurant, Jack agreed. "I hadn't eaten fast food in awhile. . . . About a half hour later, I started feeling nauseous and tried to lie down. But then I had to run to the bathroom to throw up. I felt really gross and I knew it was from the food,"[20] he remembers.

When junk food crowds out nutritious foods, the body does not get the protein, vitamins, and minerals it needs. Without quality food, the body's immune system may weaken. This can lead to repeated colds and other minor illnesses. In addition, processed junk food often has little fiber. A low-fiber diet can disrupt the digestive system and cause constipation.

Obesity on the Rise

The health effects of a junk food diet can be much more serious than a temporary upset stomach or loss of energy. In the past twenty years Americans have put on pounds at an alarming rate. According to recent studies, approximately two-thirds of Americans are overweight or obese. Doctors use a person's height and weight to calculate their body mass index (BMI). An adult is considered overweight if his or her BMI is between 25.0 and 29.9. Adults with a BMI over 30 are considered obese.

In addition, the number of overweight children aged six to eleven has more than doubled. The number of overweight

Body Mass Index Chart

Height (in)	Weight (lbs)																							
	100	105	110	115	120	125	130	135	140	145	150	155	160	165	170	175	180	185	190	195	200	205	210	215
5'0"	19	20	21	22	23	24	25	26	27	28	29	30	31	32	33	34	35	36	37	38	39	40	41	42
5'1"	18	19	20	21	22	23	24	25	26	27	28	29	30	31	32	33	34	35	36	36	37	38	39	40
5'2"	18	19	20	21	22	22	23	24	25	26	27	28	29	30	31	32	33	33	34	35	36	37	38	39
5'3"	17	18	19	20	21	22	23	24	24	25	26	27	28	29	30	31	32	32	33	34	35	36	37	38
5'4"	17	18	18	19	20	21	22	25	24	24	25	26	27	28	29	30	31	31	32	33	34	35	36	37
5'5"	16	17	18	19	20	20	21	22	23	24	25	25	26	27	28	29	30	30	31	32	33	34	35	35
5'6"	16	17	17	18	19	20	21	21	22	23	24	25	25	26	27	28	29	29	30	31	32	33	34	34
5'7"	15	16	17	18	18	19	20	21	22	22	23	24	25	25	26	27	28	29	29	30	31	32	33	33
5'8"	15	16	16	17	18	19	19	20	21	22	22	23	24	25	25	26	27	28	28	29	30	31	32	32
5'9"	14	15	16	17	17	18	19	20	20	21	22	22	23	24	25	25	26	27	28	28	29	30	31	31
5'10"	14	15	15	16	17	18	18	19	20	20	21	22	23	23	24	25	25	26	27	28	28	29	30	30
5'11"	14	14	15	16	16	17	18	18	19	20	21	21	22	23	23	24	25	25	26	27	28	28	29	30
5'12"	13	14	14	15	16	17	17	18	19	19	20	21	21	22	23	23	24	25	25	26	27	27	28	29
6'1"	13	13	14	15	15	16	17	17	18	19	19	20	21	21	22	23	23	24	25	25	26	27	27	28
6'2"	12	13	14	14	15	16	16	17	18	18	19	19	20	21	21	22	23	23	24	25	25	26	27	27
6'3"	12	13	13	14	15	15	16	16	17	18	18	19	20	20	21	21	22	23	23	24	25	25	26	26
6'4"	12	12	13	14	14	15	15	16	17	17	18	18	19	20	20	21	22	22	23	23	24	25	25	26

Underweight   Healthy   Overweight   Obese   Extremely obese

Underweight = 12–18

Normal healthy weight = 18–24

Overweight = 25–29

Obesity = 30+

Athletes and Junk Food

Eating junk food can impact athletic performance. Although athletes might get a quick burst from sugary snacks, eventually a poor diet will have a negative effect. They will experience energy swings and weight gain. Their muscles might also become slow to repair and recover. "You can exercise and train as hard as you want," says Kristine Clark, director of sports nutrition at Penn State University's Athletic Department, "but it's balanced nutrition that really determines your health and energy levels."[1]

Women's National Basketball Association star Sheryl Swoopes experienced firsthand the effects of a junk food diet. Swoopes was known for her love of junk food. She often ate doughnuts, candy bars, and fast food lunches and washed her food down with Dr. Pepper. While running during practice, Swoopes started to feel woozy and fainted on the floor. All the junk food caused Swoopes's blood sugar to dramatically surge and fall. She lacked the nutrition of lean proteins and complex carbohydrates and was also dehydrated from not drinking enough water.

The fainting episode was a wake-up call. Since then Swoopes has changed her diet. She makes healthier choices and tries to spread her nutrients and calories throughout the day in order to avoid any highs or lows. Still, Swoopes admits eating healthy is a challenge. "The hardest part is that the old stuff tastes so good, and it's so easy to get fast food," she says. "But at least now I don't eat as many doughnuts."[2]

1. Quoted in Louise Jarvis, "Great Athletes, Lousy Diets," *Women's Sports & Fitness,* April 2000.

2. Quoted in Jarvis, "Great Athletes, Lousy Diets.

adolescents aged twelve to seventeen has more than tripled. A lack of physical activity and increased portion sizes are the two main factors behind the weight gain. Many experts have also put some of the blame on a diet rich in high-calorie junk food.

A study led by researchers at Children's Hospital Boston looked at the link between obesity and fast food. One group of study participants ate fast food more than twice a week. They also watched television at least two hours daily. The second group ate fast food no more than once a week. This second group limited television watching to less than ninety minutes per day. Researchers found that the group that ate more fast food and watched more television had three times the risk of obesity and abnormal glucose levels.

Soda also fuels the extra pounds. In September 2009, researchers interviewed forty-two thousand Californians of all ages. They found that drinking one or more nondiet soda each day made adults 25 percent more likely to be overweight. "A bottle of soda is nothing more than a sugar delivery device," says Harold Goldstein, executive director of the California Center for Public Health Advocacy. "For the first time, we have strong scientific evidence that soda is one of the—if not the largest—contributors to the obesity epidemic."[21]

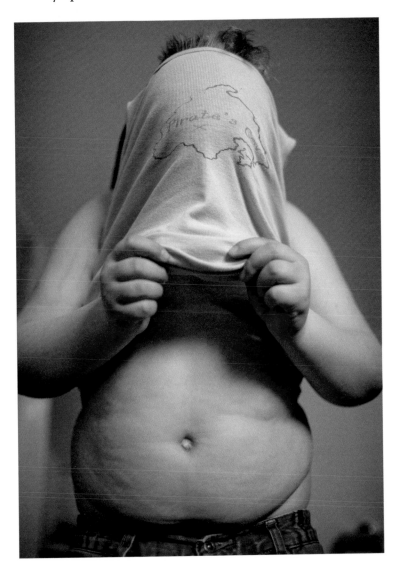

Due in part to junk food, the number of overweight children between the ages of six and eleven has more than doubled.

Those extra pounds can significantly affect health. Obese and overweight people have a higher risk of developing diabetes and heart disease. Carrying excess weight can also increase the risk of developing cancer. Scientists say that obesity and physical inactivity may be the cause of 25 to 30 percent of several types of cancer, including colon, breast, endometrial, kidney, and esophageal. The added pounds also increase the chances of having sleep apnea, bone and joint problems, gallbladder disease, and fatty liver disease. "Obesity may soon cause as much preventable disease and death as cigarette smoking,"[22] warns Ann Cea, president of the Medical Society of the State of New York.

Doctors are especially concerned about the health effects of obesity on children. "Obesity affects every organ system in a child's body, and it can do so in a much more profound way than in adults because children are still growing and developing,"[23] says David Ludwig, a pediatric endocrinologist and associate professor at Harvard Medical School. He says that obesity could reduce a child's life expectancy by two to five years. With one-third of children overweight or obese, researchers worry that this generation may be the first to live shorter lives than their parents.

> **NUTRITION FACT**
>
> **$100 billion per year**
>
> The cost of diseases associated with obesity in the United States

Heart Disease and Stroke

Junk food can be a factor in several life-threatening diseases. Heart disease is one of the most serious of these. Many junk foods have high levels of saturated fat. The unhealthy fat causes cholesterol, a soft, waxy substance, to build up on artery walls. As the cholesterol collects on the artery walls, it forms a plaque that can clog the arteries. If a blood clot gets stuck near the plaque, it can block blood flow to the heart. When this happens, a heart attack occurs. If the clot blocks blood flow to the brain, the person has a stroke.

Another type of fat, called trans fat, can also increase a person's risk of heart disease. Trans fats are created when

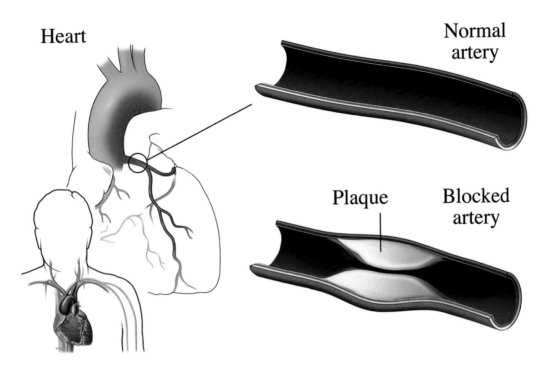

Heart

Normal artery

Plaque

Blocked artery

hydrogen is pumped into liquid oil at a high temperature. This process is called partial hydrogenation. The resulting trans fat improves the shelf life and appearance of packaged foods. It can be found in processed foods, such as cookies, pizza dough, and crackers. Many fast food restaurants also used trans fats to make their food crisp and flavorful. Research has shown, however, that trans fats are linked to an increase in bad, or LDL, cholesterol and contribute to heart disease. According to Clyde Yancy, president of the American Heart Association, a 2 percent increase in trans fat can result in a 25 percent increased risk of heart disease.

Unhealthy fat causes plaque to build up on artery walls. This can block blood flow to the heart and cause a heart attack.

Low-fat junk food might also cause heart damage. In a 2008 report, Boston University researchers followed thirteen hundred women without heart disease. They found that the women who ate lots of low-fat junk food showed a troubling sign. They had a significant increase in the thickness of their carotid artery walls. The thickened walls are a predictor of cardiovascular disease.

In addition, the high levels of salt in junk food can lead to high blood pressure, or hypertension, in some people. High blood pressure is a significant risk factor for heart disease. Over time, increased blood pressure can damage veins and arteries. It can also damage important organs and lead to strokes and kidney disease.

Type 2 Diabetes

Some people are born with diabetes. Type 1 diabetes is a condition in which the pancreas cannot produce enough insulin. The body uses insulin to break down sugars in food, which the body needs to process for energy. Type 2 diabetes occurs when the pancreas makes insulin but the body cannot use it properly.

For many years doctors considered type 2 diabetes an adult disease. Although they do not know the exact cause of this disease, doctors do know that overweight adults are at a greater risk of developing it. In recent years, however, the number of children and teens diagnosed with type 2 diabetes has steadily increased. "It's really stunning how the percentages for type 2 diabetes are going up in younger and

Medical experts blame the rise in type 2 diabetes in children on junk food, bigger portions, and less exercise.

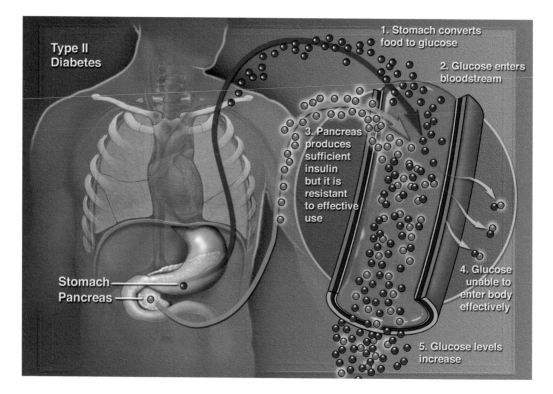

Type II Diabetes

1. Stomach converts food to glucose

2. Glucose enters bloodstream

3. Pancreas produces sufficient insulin but it is resistant to effective use

4. Glucose unable to enter body effectively

5. Glucose levels increase

Stomach

Pancreas

Okinawa Crisis

Okinawa is an island off the coast of Japan. For generations people living there ate a diet rich in soy, fish, fruits, and vegetables. The Okinawans were considered some of the healthiest people in the world and had long life spans. Many lived to be more than one hundred years old.

After World War II, however, the American military set up bases on the island. Younger Okinawans saw the American lifestyle and quickly adopted it. In 1976 McDonald's opened its first fast food restaurant on Okinawa. "This was the most delicious food I had ever eaten," Kei Sunakawa, 51, said of his first experience with McDonald's. "It was always a fun place, always filled with people."[1]

Today Okinawa has the most hamburger restaurants per person in Japan. Okinawans are also the heaviest people in Japan. Nearly half of middle-aged men are obese. In addition, their life expectancy has fallen dramatically. Nearly 30 percent of Okinawan men die before reaching age sixty-five.

One resident, Shigeru Kamizato, has stopped eating fast food. "Don't get me wrong," he said. "I still think American food is the best in the world. Things have just changed from the viewpoint of health. It's bad for you, we know now. But it's the most delicious—by far. I still love it. If there was a burger here, right here, I'd eat it."[2]

1. Quoted in Norimitsu Onishi, "Urasoe Journal; On U.S. Fast Food, More Okinawans Grow Super-Sized," *New York Times*, March 30, 2004. www.nytimes.com/2004/03/30/world/urasoe-journal-on-us-fast-food-more-okinawans-grow-super-sized.html?pagewanted=1.

2. Quoted in Onishi, "Urasoe Journal; On U.S. Fast Food, More Okinawans Grow Super-Sized."

Boys pose in front of a McDonald's in Okinawa, Japan.

younger Americans. Clearly, diabetes is following obesity, and both have huge ramifications on long-term health,"[24] says Siri Atma Greeley, a pediatric endocrinologist at the University of Chicago Medical Center.

Medical experts blame the rise in type 2 diabetes on a junk food diet, increased portion sizes, and lack of physical exercise. Over time, type 2 diabetes can cause serious health problems. Diabetics can suffer from blindness, kidney failure, amputations from loss of circulation, and cardiovascular disease. "We are already seeing some 20- and 25-year-old kids now on dialysis for kidney failure. It's chilling,"[25] says Rebecca Lipton, associate professor in pediatric endocrinology at the University of Chicago.

The Cancer Link

Some types of cancer have also been connected to junk food. Breast cancer in particular has been linked to a high-fat diet. Researchers at the National Cancer Institute studied two groups of postmenopausal women. One group ate a diet that was 40 percent fat. The other group ate a diet that was 20 percent fat. The study showed that the group who ate the higher-fat diet had a 15 percent increased risk of breast cancer. According to researcher Anne Thiebaut, "We detected a direct association between fat intake and the risk of invasive breast cancer."[26]

A major European study has also linked the high levels of sugar in junk food to cancer in women. In the study, researchers at the Umea University Hospital in Sweden followed sixty-five thousand adults over thirteen years. They found that women with elevated blood sugar levels had a significantly higher risk of developing pancreas, skin, womb, and urinary tract cancers. "The results of this research are concerning. However, the good news is that it is possible to reduce your blood sugar levels by eating a healthy balanced diet with lots of fruit and vegetables and maintaining a healthy weight,"[27] said Greg Martin, science and research manager for the World Cancer Research Fund UK. Natasha Marsland, care manager at Diabetes UK, agreed: "We know that up to 40 percent of cancer cases can be prevented by this type of healthy lifestyle, so this is just another reason for people to make those small changes that could make a big difference."[28]

Liver and Gallbladder Disease

Junk food diets rich in processed and easily digested carbohydrates can also lead to fatty liver disease. When a person eats foods high in sugar and simple carbohydrates, his or her body increases insulin production. The insulin helps convert the sugar into energy. It tells the body to make and store fat. The pancreas makes the insulin and then passes it to the liver. Eventually, too much insulin can cause a fat buildup in the liver. Fatty liver disease can lead to liver inflammation and failure.

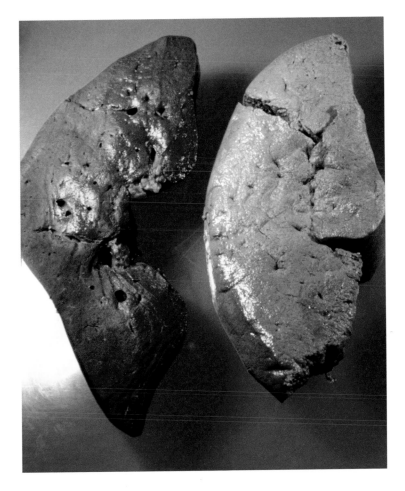

A healthy liver, left, and a fatty liver, right. The processed carbohydrates and sugars in junk food can cause fatty liver disease.

For many years liver disease occurred most often in alcoholic adults. In recent years, however, the disease has been diagnosed in children and teens. According to Brent Tetri, a leading researcher in nonalcoholic fatty liver disease, the disease affects about one in eight children in the United States. Some of these children will eventually develop serious liver disease.

To understand why fatty liver disease is on the rise, Tetri and his colleagues at the Saint Louis University Liver Center studied how a diet that was 40 percent fat and high in sugar affected mice. Tetri says:

> We wanted to mirror the kind of diet many Americans subsist on, so the high fat content is about the same you'd find in a typical McDonald's meal, and the high fructose corn syrup translates to about eight cans of soda a day in a human diet, which is not far off from what some people consume. . . . But we were also keeping the mice sedentary, with a very limited amount of activity.[29]

After sixteen weeks Tetri was surprised at how fast the diet damaged the mice's livers. "We had a feeling we'd see evidence of fatty liver disease by the end of the study," he says. "But we were surprised to find how severe the damage was and how quickly it occurred. It took only four weeks for liver enzymes to increase and for glucose intolerance—the beginning of type 2 diabetes—to begin."[30]

The refined and processed carbohydrates and sugars in junk food cause fatty liver disease, not the fat itself. Junk food such as low- or reduced-fat cookies can still cause damage. "Two low-fat Twinkies, billed as a health food, contain the same amount of sugar as an oral glucose tolerance test—a test [in which people are purposely given a large amount of sugar] to determine how much sugar someone can digest,"[31] says David Ludwig, a researcher at the Children's Hospital Boston.

NUTRITION FACT

300,000

Number of preventable deaths each year caused by physical inactivity and unhealthy eating

In addition to fatty liver disease, a junk food diet can cause gallbladder disease. The gallbladder is located directly under the liver. It holds the bile produced by the liver to digest fats. When a person eats fatty foods, the gallbladder empties its bile into the small intestine for digestion. Research has found that a diet high in refined carbohydrates can cause the body not to produce enough bile. As a result, some fats remain in large, undigested particles. They attract bacteria, which can inflame the gallbladder. In addition, undigested cholesterol can harden into gallstones and block the gallbladder's opening. Both conditions cause severe pain and can become deadly if not treated.

Sabotaging Teeth and Bones

Twenty years ago the average teen drank almost equal amounts of milk and soda. Today teens drink almost twice as much soda as milk. Experts believe that this trend is undermining healthy bones and teeth. Scientists have discovered that large amounts of fructose, the main sweetener in sodas, can disrupt the balance of minerals needed for healthy bones. As a result, soda drinkers may not absorb all the calcium they eat. This affects bone development during the critical teen years and can lead to lasting skeletal problems. For teens, two or more cans of soda daily can be enough to weaken bones. In addition, studies have found that girls who drink soda are three times more likely to break a bone than non-soda drinkers. Colas are particularly harmful. The phosphoric acid in these sodas interferes with the body's absorption of calcium and building of bone mass.

In addition, sugary drinks erode teeth. Sodas contain sugars and acids that damage tooth enamel. Enamel is a hard, white substance that protects teeth from tooth decay. When a person drinks soda or another sweetened drink, the sugar in the drink reacts with bacteria in the mouth and creates an acid. The acid attacks and erodes the enamel on teeth until it weakens and thins. Teeth with weakened enamel are more at risk for tooth decay. Even diet sodas harm teeth. Although they have less sugar, diet sodas still have similar amounts of acid as regular soda.

Super Size

In 2003 filmmaker Morgan Spurlock tried an experiment. He wanted to see just how bad junk food, particularly fast food, was for his body. For thirty days, he ate breakfast, lunch, and dinner at McDonald's restaurants. He filmed his experience for the 2004 documentary *Super Size Me*. He could not eat anything during that time that was not served at McDonald's. He also had to say yes if McDonald's employees offered to super size his meal.

In thirty days Spurlock's health quickly spiraled downward. After eating an average of 5,000 calories per day, he gained almost 25 pounds (11.3kg). His cholesterol levels skyrocketed to an unhealthy 230. He experienced mood swings, sexual problems, and liver damage.

While Spurlock expected to gain weight during the thirty-day experiment, feelings of depression and addiction surprised him. He says:

> [I got] so depressed. I think, after about a week in, I started to get really down. I would feel better when I would eat. I would eat and start to feel a little more elation, but then I'd crash and be depressed again. I think my body was starting to get very used to the high fat, high sugar diet. And then the caffeine is another big one, you're drinking that much caffeine, your body will really react to it.[32]

At one point Spurlock felt so bad that he almost quit. He recalls:

> On day 21 . . . I was really sick, and felt miserable, and I woke up in the middle of the night with massive chest pains and couldn't breathe. I was really frightened at that point. When you have three doctors who are looking at your blood tests and comparing your liver to pâté [chopped meat] . . . you're looking at these things and three doctors are saying you have to stop because they don't know what's going to happen to you. That's not the advice you want to hear. Especially when in the beginning you had three doctors who said "maybe you'll gain a little weight and your cholesterol will go up a little bit, but that's it."[33]

After the experiment, getting back in shape took a lot longer than the thirty-day junk food binge. It took Spurlock fourteen months to lose the weight and get his body back to normal. "It was tough,"[34] he admits.

Spurlock's film caused an international stir. It triggered heated debates between people about fast food. Critics claimed that Spurlock would have seen the same results on any 5,000 calorie-a-day diet. Others say the high level of fat and low level of nutrients in fast food was responsible for his deteriorating health. Spurlock says:

> For me it's about this type of all-American lifestyle, this fast food culture that has permeated our whole way of life in America. And now we've franchised out all over the world. Now we've made this great way of eating and living, where we don't think of what we're shoveling in our mouths, and don't think of the quality

Morgan Spurlock's documentary Super Size Me *showed what can happen to a person's health when he or she eats nothing but fast food for thirty days.*

of the calories that we eat. That's what's really taken over. For me, as much as I think the film is a wake up call for Americans, I think it is an immense wake up call for Europeans.[35]

Shortly after the film hit theaters, McDonald's eliminated super-size menu options. They also introduced healthier menu options like apples and salads. McDonald's denied these changes had any connection to Spurlock's film.

How Much Is Too Much?

Morgan Spurlock's experiment was extreme. Very few people eat only junk food for every meal. Some people believe that a small amount of junk food can be part of a healthy diet. Says Michelle May, author of *Eat What You Love, Love What You Eat: How to Break Your Eat-Repent-Repeat Cycle*:

> It is absolutely possible to eat junk food in moderation. To decide how much, consider not just the snack or the meal in front of you or even just that day, but consider your overall diet. For example, you may have a day where you eat mostly fast food because of your schedule. A day like that needs to be balanced with healthier-eating days. That way you consume an adequate number of nutrients overall while decreasing the quantity of less nutritious ingredients.[36]

Others disagree and say that all junk food should be avoided. In a September 2009 episode of *The Doctors*, the television show's hosts used a set of nineteen-year-old twins to demonstrate the health effects of eating junk food only one time.

To begin doctors tested twins Celina and Carolyn. Both had healthy blood counts and blood flow. Then the girls ate a meal. Celina enjoyed a high-fat, high-calorie meal. She ate chocolate cake, french fries, egg rolls, and a fried chicken sandwich. Carolyn ate a healthier meal of salmon, rice, broccoli, and salad. A few hours after eating, doctors again tested the twins. This time doctors found that Celina's triglycerides had doubled and her heart was working 30 percent harder. In comparison, Carolyn's triglycerides had remained about the same. In addition, Celina's blood sample after the fatty meal looked significantly cloudier than her pre-meal sample. According to the show's doctors, the fat in her meal had already entered her bloodstream after only a few hours.

Junk food may be tasty and convenient, but it can have lasting effects on health. Eating a diet rich in junk food increases the risk of serious disease and death.

CHAPTER 3

Hooking the Youngest Eaters

Many kids are getting hooked early on high-fat, empty-calorie junk foods. Often they find it easier to get a fast food snack than a piece of fresh fruit. Television, the Internet, and movies bombard them with advertisements for the latest candy, soda, or chip. Vending machines and à la carte lunch options at school are filled with sugar and fat. Even the youngest kids regularly eat junk food. According to a Gerber Products survey, parents allow 10 percent of toddlers aged nineteen to twenty-four months to eat candy daily. In addition, 21 percent of toddlers eat french fries daily, while 23 percent wash them down with sweetened beverages. "It's a minefield out there for kids. Schools have a big part to play, but kids often are not offered the best choices at school or in the community. It's up to parents to lead by example,"[37] says Alexandra Salazar, a pediatric nutritionist at the Children's Hospital at Montefiore in New York City.

Marketing to Kids

Marketers for junk food know children and teens influence billions of dollars of spending each year. Kids under twelve spend about $35 billion of their own money from allowances, birthday gifts, and small jobs. They also influence another

$200 billion of their parents' money. With that amount of influence, kids and teens are prime targets for junk food marketing. According to a Kaiser Family Foundation report: "This generation has become a huge consumer group that is worthy of attention from many businesses seeking to maximize their potential. Kids, teens and young adults spend significant amounts of their own money, and they influence the shopping behavior of their parents, siblings, their relatives and other adults in their lives."[38]

Junk food companies spend a lot of money on marketing aimed directly at kids. According to a Federal Trade Commission study, forty-four major food and beverage companies spent $1.6 billion in 2006 to market their products to children and adolescents in the United States. Soda companies spent the most, followed by fast food restaurants and breakfast cereal producers.

Ads for breakfast cereal and soda dominate commercials in kids' shows.

Ads on Television

Children's advertising appears on television, in print, or on the radio. Television commercials are one of the most popular ways to reach kids. Junk food companies report that they spend slightly more than half of their youth advertising budget on television ads. Ads for breakfast cereals, fast food, and soda dominate commercials in kids' shows. At the same time, ads for fruit and vegetables are hard to find. In 2006 soda makers spent about $500 million on advertising directed at kids. In comparison, fruit and vegetable growers spent about $11 million. "The vast majority of the foods that kids see advertised on television today are for products that nutritionists would tell us they need to be eating less of, not more of, if we're going to get a handle on childhood obesity,"[39] said Vicky Rideout of the Kaiser Family Foundation.

The junk food message comes to kids at a furious pace. One study counted eleven junk food commercials during one hour of Saturday morning cartoons. That is about one ad every five minutes. Researchers at the Kaiser Family Foundation say that children aged eight to twelve see the most food ads on television. They average about twenty-one ads per day. Over a year that is about seventy-six hundred ads. Teens watch about seventeen ads a day, or about six thousand a year. The youngest kids, aged two to seven, see the fewest ads. They average about twelve a day, or forty-four hundred per year.

The barrage of ads appears to be working. Kids who see junk food ads on television are more likely to ask for those foods when grocery shopping with their parents. One study tested the effect of ads on five- to eight-year-olds at summer camp. One group of children saw ads for fruit and juice. The other group viewed ads for candy and Kool-Aid beverages. Researchers found that the children were more likely to ask for the foods they had seen in commercials.

Seeing an ad only once or twice can influence a young child. One research study played a popular cartoon for groups of two- to six-year-olds. One group of kids saw the cartoon with commercials. The other group viewed the

Cartoons Promote Fruits and Vegetables

Some media companies use their characters to promote healthy foods. In 2008 PBS (Public Broadcasting Service) partnered with the Central Florida Orange County Public School District to test a new healthy eating program. District schools served elementary students veggie dippers, orange slices, stir-fry broccoli, and other fresh items not usually found in their schools. Characters from several PBS Kids' shows appeared in cafeterias to encourage kids to try the new fruit and vegetable menu items. The campaign also included contests for teachers. It rewarded classroom projects that encouraged kids to eat more fresh fruits and vegetables.

PBS also reinforces healthy eating on its Web site. Kids can play several health-themed games. Cookie Monster's Color Me Hungry teaches kids to eat a variety of colorful fruits and vegetables. Kids playing Arthur's Lunch-O-Matic help Arthur build a balanced lunch. "Encouraging families to eat right and be active is not just a one-time message and PBS KIDS is committed to helping families explore what it means to lead healthy lifestyles," said Loren Mayor, vice president of corporate partnerships at PBS.

PBS, "Produce for Kids® and PBS KIDS® Partner for a Second Year with Nationwide School-Based Healthy Eating Campaign," September 3, 2008. www.pbs.org/aboutpbs/news/20080903_produceforkids.html.

cartoon commercial free. After the show the children were shown pairs of similar products and asked to pick their favorite. The children who watched the commercials were much more likely to choose the item they saw advertised. If the child saw the ad twice, the preference for it was even stronger.

Cartoon Salespeople

Many junk food companies license familiar faces to sell their products to kids. In grocery stores products decorated with cartoon and movie characters line the shelves. Barbie dolls advertise cereal and toaster pastries. Dora the Explorer dolls appear on labels and packages for canned soups, cereals, and cookies. They appeal directly to kids, who then beg their parents to buy the character-decorated food.

Media and food companies work together to cross-promote their products. When 20th Century Fox released the movie *Ice Age: Dawn of the Dinosaurs* in the summer

A Barbie doll promotional Happy Meal from McDonald's. Many toy companies and movie studios cross-promote their products with fast food chains.

of 2009, they signed a deal with McDonald's to promote the movie. For several weeks every McDonald's Happy Meal featured *Ice Age* packaging and an *Ice Age* toy. Burger King teamed with Sony to promote *Cloudy with a Chance of Meatballs*, a fall 2009 movie based on a classic children's book. According to the Federal Trade Commission, cross-promotion tied foods and beverages to more than eighty kid-friendly movies, television shows, and cartoon characters in 2006. Characters appeared in ads in movie theaters, television, product packages, the Internet, and in-store displays. Food marketers also created special snacks, cereals, frozen waffles, and candies. They called them "limited edition items" to promote the movie or show. Other times, ads directed kids to a Web site. There they could enter to win a prize, play games, or get free downloads, such as screen savers and ringtones.

> **NUTRITION FACT**
>
> **77%**
>
> Percentage of high schools that sell soda or sweetened fruit drinks in their vending machines or school stores

Companies use cartoons and popular television and movie characters to promote their food because it attracts kids. Third-party licensing is a quick way to bring the buzz and popularity of a hit cartoon or movie to a junk food product. In addition, when a cartoon character sells a product, kids are more likely to remember the brand and its slogan. In 1996, 10 percent of fruit snacks had licensing agreements. By 2003 that number had risen to 45 percent. Sales during that time substantially increased every year.

Internet and Digital Marketing

Junk food companies have also moved online to reach children and teens. Some create kid-friendly pages on their Web sites. Others create a separate Web site just for kids and teens. These pages might feature games or cartoons. On the Nabisco Web site, Race for the Stuf is a game with Oreo cookies. The McDonald's Web site has a kids' page with games, arts and crafts, and information on the latest Happy Meal toys. When Bakugan toys were cross-promoted in Happy Meals, a child could watch the latest Bakugan Happy Meal commercial and download Bakugan coloring pages, wallpaper, and screen savers.

Food companies buy pop-up, banner, and streaming ads on other Web sites popular with kids and teens, such as Nick.com, Disney.com, and MySpace. These ads often contain links back to the food company's Web site. Some offer e-mail newsletters to keep kids up-to-date on the latest products and promotions. Other companies use podcasts and Webisodes, online videos similar to television shows, made for kids and teens. Soda companies entice teens with free downloadable ring tones in their caps or labels.

Online advertising lets food companies reach more kids and teens at a smaller cost. In one example, Coca-Cola teamed with Facebook, a popular social networking site, to introduce Sprite Sips characters. Facebook users could then create their own personal characters and share them with friends on the network. Coca-Cola paid for the initial ad, but not as the characters passed from user to user. "The cost of reaching and engaging a lot more kids is a lot less than the cost of what it is to buy a 30-second television ad," said Kathryn Montgomery, American University communications professor. "With social networking, marketers are getting the kids to create the ads and share them with their friends."[40]

Celebrity Endorsements

In addition to cartoons and movie characters, food and drink marketers sign up real-life celebrities to promote their products. Former Dallas Cowboys running back Emmitt Smith has appeared in ads for McDonald's and Frito-Lay. International soccer star David Beckham stars in Pepsi commercials.

The Food Commission, a UK consumer campaign group, issued a report that criticized celebrities for promoting high-sugar, high-fat junk food. "Perhaps David Beckham wore off the 55 grams of sugar calories in the half litre Pepsi he promoted during his extensive training sessions—but it won't prove so easy for your average office worker or schoolchild,"[41] the commission wrote.

To promote their products, food and drink companies often sign up celebrities, who are some children's role models. Here, soccer star David Beckham is seen on Pepsi cans.

NETTO 330 mL

Banning Junk Food Ads

Several countries around the world have taken steps to limit children's exposure to junk food ads. In the United Kingdom, ads for foods high in fat, sugar, and salt are banned during or in between television shows aimed at kids under sixteen. In Australia most popular characters were banned from television ads during kids' shows effective January 1, 2010. Ads for unhealthy food and drinks in France must carry a health warning. If they do not, advertisers pay a fine.

In the United States in 2006, ten of the largest food and drink manufacturers agreed on voluntary guidelines. These companies include General Mills, McDonald's, and Coca-Cola. They agreed that half of their advertising to children under twelve years old would market healthy food or encourage a healthy lifestyle. They also agreed not to advertise food and drinks in elementary schools. They pledged to reduce their use of third-party licensed characters in junk food ads.

Some criticize this self-enforced agreement. They claim too many loopholes exist. For example, General Mills might pull ads for Trix cereal from children's programming, but it

Getting Extreme over Junk Food

MeMe Roth, a Manhattan parent, is no stranger to the junk food controversy. The unhealthy snacks that her children see for every birthday, holiday, and celebration anger her. "I thought I was sending my kid to P.S. 9 [Public School 9], not Chuck E. Cheese," says Roth. "Is there or is there not an obesity and diabetes epidemic in this country?"[1]

Some feel that Roth's methods to keep her kids junk-food free, however, are extreme. She has lobbied for permission slips for any food not on the school lunch menu. Roth has sent heated e-mail messages to the school. At one meeting the principal said that Roth appeared very hostile, threw candy on the desk, and cursed. She also said that it was not the first time Roth had behaved that way.

At her children's previous school in New Jersey, Roth campaigned against bagels and potato chips served at lunch. In 2007 police were called to a YMCA when Roth took the sprinkles and syrups from the ice cream sundae table. She also actively campaigned against Girl Scout cookies and claimed that the organization should not promote unhealthy eating. "She has some valid points, but the way she delivers them is abrasive,"[2] said Jim Stanek, a fellow parent.

1. Quoted in Susan Dominus, "Mother's Fight Against Junk Food Puts a School on Edge," *New York Times*, June 15, 2009. www.nytimes.com/2009/06/16/nyregion/16bigcity.html?_r=1.

2. Quoted in Dominus, "Mother's Fight Against Junk Food Puts a School on Edge."

could still advertise Trix during family shows. In addition, cereals like Cocoa Puffs, which have less sugar but are still less healthy, could still be advertised on children's shows.

For some the voluntary guidelines are not strong enough. They want junk food ads banned entirely. "Just as you wouldn't expect to see a tobacco ad on a kids' site or show, there shouldn't be junk food ads there either,"[42] says Fahmida Rashid, a thirty-one-year-old mother in Brooklyn, New York. Others, however, such as Chris Chapman, chair of the Australian Communications and Media Authority (ACMA), believe the issue is not so clear-cut. "The ACMA concludes that the relative contribution of advertising to childhood obesity is difficult to quantify and that a causal relationship between these may not be possible to determine," he says. "In addition, there is only limited evidence about the benefits of banning food and beverage advertising, as this is an area where research is only beginning to emerge internationally and locally."[43]

Food Choices at School

Even at school, children and teens are often surrounded by junk food choices. Most schools provide food and drinks to their students under the National School Lunch Program. Food sold under this program must meet U.S. Department of Agriculture (USDA) nutrition standards. School lunches must have no more than 30 percent of calories from fat and 10 percent of calories from saturated fat. In addition, school lunches should provide one-third of the Recommended Dietary Allowance for protein, vitamin A, vitamin C, iron, calcium, and calories. Foods defined as having minimum nutritional value, such as gum, soda, and jelly beans, cannot be served inside the school cafeteria during mealtimes. Schools that follow these guidelines receive reimbursements from the federal government.

Many schools do offer healthy options with school lunches.

While following the standards, each school can choose the types of foods to serve and how they are prepared. In 2009 a School Nutrition Association survey found that many schools do offer healthy options with school lunches. Almost all schools offered fat-free or low-fat milk, fresh fruits and vegetables, and whole-grain items. In addition, 91 percent of schools offered a salad bar or pre-packaged salad option to students. "These survey results show that despite the difficult economy, school nutrition professionals nationwide continue to provide children with high quality, nutritious foods and educate them on making the right food choices,"[44] stated School Nutrition Association president Dora Rivas.

Competitive Foods

If a student were to eat all parts of the USDA school lunch every day, he or she would have a nutritionally sound diet. In reality, however, most students choose other food options. In addition to school lunches, many schools offer other foods and drinks to students. Vending machines sell soda, sports drinks, chips, and high-fat packaged foods. School stores and snack bars offer candy and cookies. Even the lunchroom itself can serve less healthy foods such as french fries, cake, hamburgers, and pizza as à la carte menu items. These competitive foods are not part of a USDA school meal program. They do not need to meet any federal nutrition standards.

Other loopholes in the School Lunch Program also exist. Guidelines state that soda cannot be sold in the lunchroom during mealtime. A student, however, could buy a soda from a vending machine in the hallway. In addition, some junk foods, such as doughnuts and cookies, are made with fortified flour. Under the guidelines they are not considered foods of minimal nutritional value simply because they include the fortified flour. Schools can sell these popular items next to the fruits and vegetables.

When given the option, many kids choose junk food at school. A survey of 228 Pennsylvania high schools found that the top-selling à la carte items were hamburgers, pizza, and sandwiches. Cookies, crackers, cakes, and pastries were also popular. In school stores that sold food, candy was the

top seller. Kate Wilson, president of the School Nutrition Association, says that kids choose french fries, candy bars, chips, and soda because they like the way these foods taste. "Unless kids are properly educated, they're going to choose junk over healthy food at school and at home,"[45] says Wilson.

In spite of healthier lunches, school vending machines still offer candy bars, soda, and chips.

Why Not Pull the Plug?

Some people think schools should get rid of the vending machines and stop selling junk food to students. For school administrators, however, the answer is not that easy. "Schools lose money every day because it costs more money to prepare meals than the reimbursement they get from the federal government,"[46] says Donald Schumacher, medical director for the Center for Nutrition and Preventive Medicine in Charlotte, North Carolina. He says that in 2008 the government reimbursed schools $2.57 per meal per student. For many schools, however, the cost to prepare the meals was higher. For some the cost was $2.68 per meal. That eleven-cent deficit adds up quickly. A school with one thousand students would lose $19,800 a year. Multiplied by 29.6 million children in the National School Lunch Program, the deficit across the country would be $3.2 million per day.

Offering competitive foods that do not meet USDA guidelines is one way schools make money. "Without full funding from the government, schools are being pinched, and *we* need a quick way to make money," says Wilson. "That's why we have vending machines. That's why we sell à la carte. And that's why we purchase unhealthy foods along with healthy foods. They're cheaper than the healthier foods, and we can turn a greater profit."[47]

Pouring Rights at School

In addition to selling junk food, some schools have signed pouring rights contracts with soft drink companies. The soft drink companies pay school districts for the right to sell only their products in school vending machines and at all school events. The soft drink companies benefit from exclusive access to the students. They display logos on vending machines, cups, sportswear, brochures, and even in the halls of school buildings. The soda companies hope this exposure will build brand loyalty in students for the rest of their lives.

At first these types of contracts were common on college and high school campuses. However, they have expanded to elementary and middle schools in some districts. By 2007 a majority of schools had exclusive marketing agreements with soft drink companies—almost 75 percent of high schools, 65 percent of middle schools, and 30 percent of elementary schools.

Most pouring rights contracts pay schools a large up-front payment with additional payments over a five- to ten-year period. The payments provide needed money for schools. They often fund sports, arts, or computer facilities. In Wisconsin, the Racine Unified School District struggled through years of budget problems, school closings, and teacher layoffs. In 2000 the district decided to sign a ten-year marketing agreement with PepsiCo. In return, they received an up-front payment of $450,000 and an annual payment of about $200,000. In Oregon a larger school district received an up-front payment of $1.2 million from Coca-Cola.

In response to public pressure to improve school nutrition, several large soft drink companies, including Coca-Cola and PepsiCo, and the American Beverage Association agreed to limit soda sales in schools beginning in 2009. "It's time to get the soda and the junk food out, and even the industry now, the junk food industry, recognizes that times have changed and they have to change, too,"[48] said Connecticut senator Donald Williams.

Schools, however, are finding it hard to implement the new agreement and pull high-sugar drinks out of school vending machines. Many pouring rights contracts have penalties if the schools stop selling soft drinks or change

Many schools are stuck in old contracts with soda companies and cannot afford to move them. One Oregon school district received $1.2 million from Coca-Cola.

the mix of drinks in vending machines. When the Oregon school district wanted to remove diet soda and sports drinks from their vending machines, they discovered they would have to pay a six-hundred-thousand-dollar penalty. In the Racine, Wisconsin, school district, officials decided to wait until their marketing contract expired in 2010 before removing high-calorie drinks from their schools. They could not afford to pay the two-hundred-thousand-dollar fine. "Many school districts are stuck with a deal with the devil. . . . The schools could buy out the contract, but this is about kids and school districts that are strapped for cash,"[49] said Deborah Pinkas, a Portland lawyer who wrote a study on beverage contracts.

Push for Healthier Choices

Alarmed by the rise in junk food eating, many people urge schools to offer healthier foods in all areas. In 2007 the Institute of Medicine issued guidelines for school foods, including competitive foods. They recommended that schools only sell apples, carrot sticks, raisins, yogurt, and other low-fat and nonfat snacks with no more than 30 grams of added sugar. Candy bars, potato chips, and snacks with trans fats or 35 percent of calories from fat should be cut. For drinks, they recommended only water, low-fat milk, and limited amounts of 100 percent juices. In addition, the report suggested that teachers stop using food as rewards for students. It also called for food in classroom celebrations to follow nutritious guidelines.

Although nutritionists applaud the report, they worry that recommendations will do little to force schools to change. "It's not going to make a difference or do any good if these standards aren't implemented," said Janey Thornton, president of the School Nutrition Association and director of child-nutrition programs for the fourteen-thousand-student district in Hardin County, Kentucky. "There are already many schools that have made great strides in changing what

> ## NUTRITION FACT
>
> ### 200 calories
>
> Number of calories Americans eat more per day than ten years ago

is sold in vending machines and other venues in the school system, but there are still going to be many schools that won't ever change unless it is mandated."[50]

Children are some of the most impressionable consumers. Strong evidence exists that bombarding kids with junk food at home and school has a direct influence on what they choose to eat. Nutritionists urge parents to learn how marketers target children and what food choices their school offers. By talking to children about the differences between junk food and healthier choices, parents can help their children develop lifelong healthy eating habits.

Schools have begun offering healthier alternatives in their vending machines, such as milk and juice.

CHAPTER 4

Taking Responsibility

s the negative health effects of junk food have gotten more attention, many people have debated who is to blame for the rise in junk food eating. At the simplest level an individual decides if he or she is going to eat junk food. People control what types of food they eat and how often they put junk food in their mouths. For the youngest children, parents are an important influence and role model for eating.

With chronic conditions like obesity and type 2 diabetes on the rise, the health-care system is becoming overloaded and expensive for all. In a 2009 joint report from the United Health Foundation, the American Public Health Association, and the Partnership for Prevention, researchers calculated that obesity will cost Americans about $344 billion in medical expenses by 2018, which will be about 21 percent of total health-care spending. Many believe these expenses are preventable. They say the cost of health care could be reduced if people made healthier food choices and lost weight.

Despite health warnings, however, many still eat too much junk food. When this happens, some people believe that others should step in and place limits on junk food eating. This has caused families, schools, companies, and governments to debate their roles and responsibilities in the junk food wars.

Responsibility Starts at Home

Parents play the most influential role in a child's eating habits. In one study 120 preschoolers bought food from a play grocery store. At the same time, their parents filled out questionnaires about their shopping and eating habits. Researchers found that the children who filled their carts with sweets, sugary drinks, and salty snacks had parents who did the same. Children who filled their cart with more healthy food generally came from homes where parents also made healthier food choices. The results suggest that even children as young as two years old form food preferences,

Parents play the most influential role in a child's eating habits.

Comparing Thirst Quenchers

There are many choices to quench thirst, but nutritional values can vary greatly. Compare the following drinks:

- Soda: Most 12-ounce cans have 150 calories, most of which are from added sugar. Many also contain caffeine.
- Sports drinks: Although sports drinks often have fewer calories than sodas, they still have many added sugars.
- Juices: Even 100 percent juice can still be high in calories, so moderation is important. They do, however, provide some vitamins and calcium.
- Milk: This drink is fortified with calcium and vitamin D. The protein in milk also helps to make the stomach feel fuller longer.
- Iced coffee: These trendy drinks can pack high calories and caffeine. A McDonald's medium vanilla iced coffee has 180 calories.
- Fruit smoothies: Beware of smoothies not made with real fruit. Even those with real fruit can be high calorie, especially those made with added sugar.
- Water: Health experts consider water to be the best thirst quencher. It hydrates the body quickly without added fat, sugar, or salt.

and their parents' choices influence them. "The data suggest that children begin to assimilate and mimic their parents' food choices at a very young age, even before they are able to fully appreciate the implications of these choices,"[51] wrote the researchers in their report.

Teaching children healthy eating habits, however, is not easy. Parents struggle to balance work, after-school activities, and hectic lives. Many families skip home-cooked meals for faster, less nutritious alternatives. In addition, some families find fresh foods are too expensive. A 2009 study by Canada's Heart and Stroke Foundation found that 47 percent of Canadians do not buy fresh fruit, vegetables, dairy, whole grains, lean meats, and fish because of the cost. "A lot of parents don't want to struggle with the issues so they give up, letting kids make their own choices," says Jane Rees, director of nutrition service/education in adolescent medicine at the University of Washington School of Medicine and Public Health. "But children's judgment is less mature and they still depend on parents to guide them."[52]

Australian parenting author and columnist Duncan Fine believes that parents hold the ultimate responsibility for how much junk food their kids eat. "Kids don't have any money. Just ask my two sons. They'll tell you that I'm the one with the wallet. . . . I decide what they eat and no amount of pestering is going to change that. It's called parental responsibility and sometimes it's spelt 'Capital N, Capital O,'"[53] he says.

By the time kids become teenagers, however, they have already formed many of their food preferences. Parents have less control over what they eat. Nutritionist Laurie Beebe thinks that parents need to stay involved, especially when they have less control. She says: "Parents don't always consider that they *can* make the rules about food. I tell parents teaching healthy eating habits is like keeping your kids from smoking! They say, 'I hate to deprive Janie when she loves ice cream and cookies so much' but I ask them, 'If Janie *really really* wanted to smoke or drink wine would you tell her okay so you didn't disappoint her?'"[54]

Unlike some teens, fifteen-year-old Elyse May has taken responsibility for her eating. Three years ago she changed her diet. Now she eats vegetarian food and tries to limit the junk food she eats. She packs her own lunch for school to avoid unhealthy cafeteria options. She also works in the kitchen with her parents to create healthy, flavorful recipes. She has even published her own cookbook for teens, *Veggie Teens: A Cookbook and Guide for Vegetarian Teenagers*. Elyse finds that her friends have become more interested in healthy eating after watching her example. "They are often jealous of the variety of healthy lunches I bring, like taco salads, veggie sandwiches, pasta salad, cheese and crackers and other fresh foods,"[55] she says.

Blaming Food Companies

Some people, however, feel the blame for this generation of junk food addicts lies with the food companies themselves.

"There's a lot of people who benefit from people being fat and sick, and the whole setup is designed to make people eat more," said Marion Nestle, New York University nutrition and food sciences professor. "You're asking people to control what they eat when the food industry spends $30 billion and more on marketing designed to make them eat more."[56]

In August 2002 the parents of two teenagers filed a lawsuit against McDonald's. Nineteen-year-old Jazlyn Bradley stood 5 feet 6 inches (167.6cm) and weighed 270 pounds (122.5kg).

She said that she regularly ate a McMuffin for breakfast and a Big Mac meal for dinner. Fourteen-year-old Ashley Pelman was 4 feet 10 inches (147.3cm) tall and weighed 170 pounds (77kg). She said that she ate McDonald's Happy Meals about three to four times a week. Both girls suffered from several health problems, including obesity, heart disease, diabetes, high blood pressure, and high cholesterol levels.

The lawsuit against McDonald's claimed that the fast food restaurant did not clearly disclose the ingredients and effects of its food. Bradley's father said he never saw an ingredient list at the fast food restaurant. "I always believed McDonald's was healthy for my children,"[57] he said in an affidavit. Because most of the food on the McDonald's menus is high in fat, salt, and sugar, the lawsuit argued that McDonald's was responsible for the teens' health problems.

Ultimately, a judge tossed the McDonald's lawsuit out of court. In his ruling Judge Robert Sweet said: "If a person knows or should know that eating copious orders of super-sized McDonalds' products is unhealthy and may result in

How Much Exercise Does It Take to Burn Off a Typical McDonald's Meal?

Food	Calories	Fat (grams)	Sodium (mg)	Sugar (grams)
Quarter Pounder with Cheese	510	26	1,190	9
Large Fries	500	25	350	0
Large Coke	310	0	20	86
Total	1,320	51	1,560	95

In order to burn off a single meal, a 160-pound (72.6kg) person would have to do one of the following activities:

· Do high-impact aerobics for two hours and forty minutes.

· Run at 6 miles (9.66km) per hour for almost two hours.

· Walk at 4 miles (6.44km) per hour for about three and a half hours.

weight gain . . . it is not the place of the law to protect them from their own excesses. Nobody is forced to eat at McDonalds."[58]

For some the McDonald's lawsuit and other similar suits against fast food restaurants are an example of a legal system out of control. In 2004 the House of Representatives passed a bill that outlawed lawsuits brought by obese people against fast food restaurants. "Trial lawyers have targeted the fast-food industry as the next big tobacco by bringing these insane lawsuits," said the bill's author, Representative Ric Keller from Florida. "We've got to get back to those old-fashioned principles of personal responsibility, of common sense, and get away from this new culture where everybody plays the victim and blames other people for their problems."[59]

Food Companies Expand Offerings

Negative publicity from lawsuits and research studies has put pressure on fast food and junk food companies. In response, some have changed their menus. While the usual hamburgers and milkshakes are still available, some have expanded their menus to include healthier options.

In 2004 McDonald's revamped its Happy Meal to offer low-fat milk and apple slices choices. They also added several salads, yogurt, fruit, and grilled chicken sandwiches to the menu. Other fast food restaurants followed and introduced more healthy choices.

Frito-Lay is one of the world's largest producers of snack foods. It is the company behind the popular Doritos, Fritos, Cheetos, and Tostitos brands. After scientists proved that trans fats are unhealthy, Frito-Lay stopped using these fats in their chips in 2002.

Now Frito-Lay is trying to make its products even healthier. They use more unsaturated fats in their products instead of saturated fats that are linked to heart disease. Unsaturated fats can help lower bad (LDL) cholesterol levels and may

NUTRITION FACT

20% to 25%

Percentage of the U.S. population that eat in some kind of fast food restaurant daily

In 2004, McDonald's introduced healthier food items, such as the Chicken McGrill, salads, and a fruit and yogurt parfait.

raise HDL, or good cholesterol. "We're telling customers that it may seem counterintuitive, but there are good fats, and the fat you are going to get in our products is going to be beneficial,"[60] says Bob Brown, Frito-Lay's director of nutrition and regulatory affairs.

Choosing to use unsaturated fats was not easy for the company. The best option, sunflower oil, was in short supply. After several years and millions of dollars, however, Frito-Lay established a supply chain for the oil with farmers and oil makers. Now company researchers are looking into ways to add more whole grains and the antioxidant lycopene to products.

Despite Frito-Lay's efforts to make their products healthier, nutritionists are skeptical. "Nobody got heart disease from a deficiency of chips," says Lisa Young, a dietitian at New York University. "I think the food industry gets an A in marketing. But this is better than nothing."[61]

Employers Take Charge at Work

Some employers have decided to take their own action against junk food. Employees at the law firm Littler Mendelson in San Francisco usually feasted on trays of Krispy Kreme doughnuts, sweet rolls, and large muffins. Suzanne Perez, the firm's human resources chief, decided to pull the plug on the junk food. Now the lawyers at firm breakfasts find

Not All Hamburgers Are Created Equal

The hamburger is one of the most popular foods in America. Each year, Americans eat about 40 billion burgers, or about 150 per person. In addition, burgers are growing in size. In 1950 the average burger had a little more than 1 ounce (28.3g) of meat. Today the average burger weighs around 6 ounces (170g). In addition, restaurants have played on Americans' love of burgers to invent the double- or triple-patty burger, which piles more meat, fat, and calories on the plate. Today's burgers vary widely in their calorie and fat counts. Check out the differences between the following burgers:

- TGI Friday's Cheesy Bacon Cheeseburger: 1,590 calories and unknown grams of fat
- Red Robin A-1 Peppercorn Burger: 1,443 calories and 97 grams of fat
- Dairy Queen ½ lb. Flame Thrower GrillBurger: 1,060 calories and 75 grams of fat
- Wendy's Quarter Pound Single: 430 calories and 20 grams of fat
- McDonald's Quarter Pounder: 410 calories and 19 grams of fat

Nutrition Facts

Serving Size 1 Doughnut (52g)
Servings Per Container

Amount Per Serving

Calories 200   Calories from Fat 110

	% Daily Value*
Total Fat 12g	18%
Saturated Fat 3g	15%
Cholesterol 5mg	1%
Sodium 95mg	4%
Total Carbohydrate 22g	7%
Dietary Fiber less than 1g	2%
Sugars 10g	
Protein 2g	

Vitamin A 0%	•	Vitamin C 2%
Calcium 6%	•	Iron 4%

NET WT. 9.9 OZ (280g)

Krispy Kreme

DOUGHNUTS®

al Glazed Doughnuts

OUGHNUTS & COFFEE SINCE 1937

hard-boiled eggs, yogurt, mini quiches, cottage cheese, and fresh fruit. Perez admits, however, that her move to healthier food is not going to win any office popularity contests.

At Yamaha in Buena Park, California, human resources executive Carol Baker has exchanged the regular shipments of pies for organic fruit. She has also ordered the delivery of healthy sandwiches and salads to the company to entice people away from nearby fast food restaurants.

Some firms use price to make healthy food more appealing. At equipment manufacturer Caterpillar, the company cafeteria lowered the price of garden burgers to one dollar. They sold five times more garden burgers than they did when the burgers had a higher price. At mortgage company Freddie Mac, a worker who orders six healthy meals in the cafeteria earns a free meal. Other companies, such as Dow Corning and Sprint Nextel, charge more for unhealthy food than healthy food in their lunchrooms. "We're trying to change people's behaviors,"[62] says Yamaha's Carol Baker.

Some employers are encouraging their employees to be healthier and not bring in treats such as muffins or Krispy Kreme doughnuts.

Voluntary Guidelines

In 2008 the International Council of Beverages Associations announced voluntary guidelines for marketing to children. Companies like Coca-Cola and PepsiCo have agreed to stop advertising and marketing beverages, including soda, to children under twelve years old. The guidelines do not cover water, juice, and dairy-based drinks. The voluntary marketing guidelines are similar to measures adopted in 2006 by several major food companies. Susan Neely, president and CEO of the American Beverage Association, explains:

> The non-alcoholic beverage industry produces a wide variety of beverages, all of which can be part of a healthy lifestyle. . . . However, as parents and grandparents ourselves, we recognize that children may be more susceptible to marketing campaigns and may not always be able to make the right dietary choices for themselves. Parents are telling us they want to be the gatekeepers. We are listening and want to protect their role so that we can work together to help teach children around the world how to make more informed choices.[63]

Although some companies follow the voluntary restrictions on marketing to children, each interprets the guidelines differently. As a result, there are no consistent standards.

Critics point out that companies have too much room to get around the voluntary guidelines. Susan Linn, director of the Campaign for a Commercial Free Childhood, points to Coca-Cola's product placement on the hit show *American Idol* as an example. "It's consistently a top rated program for 2-to-11 year olds and the show is really about Coca-Cola. All these companies really make their guidelines based on their products and not what's best for kids and there's nobody to enforce it so it's hard to see that it's going to make a difference," says Linn. She adds: "Self regulation in this country hasn't been working. It still looks like lots of products are being marketed to kids that shouldn't be. And they're marketed in ways to kids that aren't even covered in the guidelines. I'm not optimistic that this is going to do much."[64]

Government's Role in Advertising

For some people self-regulation and personal responsibility is not enough. They have called for the government to regulate junk food, similarly to the way it restricts sales of tobacco and alcohol. In March 2009 Congress called for several government studies on food marketing and childhood obesity for children under eighteen years old. The goal is to determine whether the government should set standards for determining which foods are healthy and appropriate to market to children. Some groups, such as the Federal Trade Commission, applaud the studies as a first step toward developing uniform standards on food marketing to kids.

Other countries have already passed regulations on junk food sales and marketing. In France ads for unhealthy foods and drinks must also carry health messages. If they do not, the advertisers must pay a fine equal to 1.5 percent of the cost of the ad. Ireland has banned all television ads for sweets and fast food. The Irish have also banned companies from using celebrities and sports stars to promote junk food to kids. Latvia has completely banned the sale of junk food in schools and day cares. This includes any food or drink that has artificial colors, sweeteners, preservatives, or caffeine. Sweden and Norway also prohibit junk food ads for children under twelve years old. In 2007 the United Kingdom banned all television junk food ads for children under sixteen. To date, the effectiveness of these bans is unknown, since researchers are just beginning to study the area.

Countries such as Canada have shown that they are serious about junk food laws. Quebec has a law banning junk food advertising to children under thirteen. When snack cake maker Saputo Inc. ran a campaign with a cartoon gorilla in Quebec day care centers, it received a fine of forty-four thousand dollars. "Using children to sell products goes against the law. Since we cannot act on the content of food offered to children, we can at least reduce their exposure to

> **NUTRITION FACT**
>
> **45%**
> Number of Americans who said they eat junk food when feeling down

this advertising,"[65] said Suzie Pellerin, director of an anti-obesity group.

Banning Trans Fats

Several local governments have taken steps to reduce unhealthy trans fats in restaurants and bakeries. In December 2006 New York City became the first American city to ban trans fats in restaurants. Other cities and regions, such

In 2006 New York City became the first American city to ban trans fats.

as Philadelphia, Pennsylvania; Stamford, Connecticut; and Montgomery County, Maryland, have also banned trans fats. In July 2008 California became the first state to ban trans fats beginning in 2010 for restaurants and 2011 for retail bakeries. Under the new law, restaurants, bakeries, delis, and cafeterias cannot use any ingredients, such as margarine or shortening, that contain trans fats. Violators of the law will face fines that begin at twenty-five dollars but can increase to one thousand dollars.

Critics say that laws banning trans fats are unnecessary. Companies such as Wendy's, KFC, Taco Bell, the Cheesecake Factory, and McDonald's have already begun to eliminate trans fats due to customer pressure. "We don't think that a municipal health agency has any business banning a product the Food and Drug Administration has already approved,"[66] said Dan Fleshler, a spokesperson for the National Restaurant Association. In addition, restaurants claim that using different oils will be more expensive. "The only effect it is going to have on the consumer is that we are going to have to raise our prices,"[67] said Tina Pantazis, the manager of Dino's Burgers in California. She said that the price of Dino's french fries would probably jump from $1.75 to at least $2.75.

Junk Food Tax

Some believe the government should take junk food regulation even further. Legislators implemented taxes on cigarettes to reduce smoking. Increasingly, public health officials are supporting a similar tax on junk food and drinks. A junk food tax could influence people to eat less junk food. Even if it does not have this effect, the added tax could help pay for health care needed to treat conditions related to eating too much junk food. In July 2009 the Urban Institute in Washington, D.C., proposed a 10 percent tax on food of little nutritional value. It claimed the tax could raise $500 billion over ten years.

A junk food tax would also reduce or eliminate the price difference between healthy food and junk food. Junk food is often cheaper than fresh fruit, vegetables,

and meat. Taxing junk food would raise its price. Then a candy bar could cost the same as an apple. Equal prices might convince more people to ignore junk food and choose healthier options.

Are Taxes Effective?

According to research, taxes can change behavior. The Centers for Disease Control and Prevention estimates that an increase in the price of cigarettes by 10 percent reduces consumption by 4 percent. "The research around tobacco has shown that large increases in taxes on cigarettes has been the single most effective policy to reduce tobacco use," said Mary Story, a dietitian and professor at the University of Minnesota. Many believe this success can also happen with a junk food tax. "A 10 percent increase in the price of a sugar-sweetened beverage could reduce consumption,"[68] says Story.

Critics, however, say that a junk food tax will have little effect on people's eating behaviors. "This is the most ridiculous idea I've heard," said Kellie Glass, a registered dietitian in Ashland, Kentucky. "Folks are just not going to give up all the foods they love, even if they are more expensive."[69] Critics also point out that junk food taxes would hit poor people the hardest. In addition, the success with tobacco taxes might not happen with junk food. Tax cigarettes and smokers can either pay or quit. Tax a soda, however, and people can switch to unhealthy sports drinks or sweetened juices, which may have even more sugar and calories. In addition, a junk food tax would be difficult to implement. Defining which foods to tax would be subjective. For example, in Maine, a 5.5 percent snack tax was applied to blueberry muffins and fresh apple pies. English muffins and frozen pies, however, were not taxed.

Even though it would be hard to implement, support for a junk food tax is rising in the United States. A July 2009 Kaiser Foundation survey on health-care issues found that 55 percent of Americans favor a tax on unhealthy foods. Fifty-three percent support a tax on soda and other sugary soft drinks.

Despite rising public support for junk food taxes, groups such as Americans Against Food Taxes are vocal about their disagreement. In a television ad, the group states: "Taxes never made anyone healthy. Education, exercise and balanced diets do that."[70]

Despite the arguments over junk food responsibility, the decision to eat junk food is often an individual choice. People who are not well informed about the risks of junk food may not be motivated to make healthier choices. Without education, the efforts from government, businesses, and schools may have little impact on junk food behavior.

CHAPTER 5

Are You a Junk Food Junkie?

Junk food can fast become an addictive habit. Making healthier choices, however, can improve how a person feels and performs physically and mentally. Fresh foods, such as fruits, vegetables, lean meats, and low-fat dairy, are more nutritionally dense. They cut hunger faster and make a person feel full longer than empty junk food. Understanding how to make healthy food choices and create good behaviors around food are key components of kicking the junk food habit.

Eating Too Much Junk Food?

The best way to analyze a diet is to keep a food journal for a week. After each meal or snack, record the food and drink. Estimating portion sizes and then using a food calculator to determine calorie and fat counts is also helpful. Many people find that writing down everything they eat and drink is eye-opening. After keeping track of food for a week, a person can think about the following questions:

- How many times did a person eat or drink junk food, fast food, or soda? How does that compare to the number of fruits and vegetables eaten during the week?

- Is there a pattern to the junk food eating? Are there similar times of the day, such as after school or during lunch, when junk food eating happened?
- If the food was from a fast food restaurant, could healthier menu items have been chosen?
- What types of food are available in the refrigerator and pantry? Are there packages of junk food or trays of fresh fruits and vegetables?

According to registered dietician Kristen Rudolph, "The easiest way to know if you are eating healthy is to count up the food groups at each meal." She says that breakfast should have three—a protein, grain, and fruit or vegetable. For lunch and dinner, adults and teens should choose a protein, dairy, grain, and two fruits or vegetables. "Chances are if they are all there, you're doing it,"[71] says Rudolph.

The best way to analyze a diet and know whether you are eating too much junk food is to keep a food journal.

Education Is Important

If a person does not know the difference between a high-fat burger at McDonald's and a lower-fat salad, then it is difficult to make healthier food choices. Education and understanding the right balance of foods to eat are important. Most experts agree on the following guidelines for eating healthy:

1. Eat a variety of foods to get a balanced mix of all the nutrients the body needs.
2. Eat more fruits and vegetables and less animal products.
3. Eat more fresh and homemade foods and fewer processed and packaged foods.
4. Cut down on saturated and trans fats, especially those in whole-fat dairy products, fried foods, processed snack foods, and baked goods with trans fats. Unsaturated fats that are part of a healthy diet come from fish and nuts.
5. Choose food with complex carbohydrates. Cut down on the simple sugars of sodas and foods made with highly refined white flour. Instead, choose foods that list whole grain as the first ingredient.
6. Eat or drink about three cups of nonfat or low-fat dairy products each day. Calcium is especially important in the bone-building teen years.
7. Eat protein in moderation. Choose lean proteins like fish and skinless chicken.
8. Limit daily sodium intake. Stop adding table salt to foods and cut back on canned, processed foods that are high in salt.

Dietician Kristen Rudolph works with children and teens at the Children's Hospital of Pittsburgh and knows that simple rules work best to help kids and teens avoid junk food. She tells her patients to create a healthy plate at each meal. Half the plate should be full of fruits and vegetables, one quarter with lean protein and the last quarter with whole grains. She also recommends the 5-10 rule for snacking. Healthier choices should have less than 5 grams of total fat per serving and less than 10 grams of sugar per serving.

Reading Food Labels

In 1990 federal regulation required food companies to put nutrition information on their food in a standardized way. Nutrition Facts labels tell people how big a serving size is and how many servings are in a package. They also provide information about the amount of calories, fat, carbohydrates, sodium, fiber, sugars, and protein in the food. Labels also give the amount of any vitamins or minerals in the food. A second

Nutrition Facts labels provide information on the number of calories and amount of fat as well as other nutritional information.

column on the label calculates the percentage of the recommended daily value for a nutrient. For example, a 1.5-ounce (42.5g) box of raisins contains 33 grams of carbohydrates, or 11 percent of the recommended daily value. In addition, food labels list ingredients in the food. The list is ordered from greatest to least. On a box of Froot Loops breakfast cereal, the ingredient used the most and listed first is sugar.

Some food labels, however, are misleading. In addition to the required Nutrition Facts label, food manufacturers can print claims like "low fat," "reduced," or "light" on packaging. Sometimes, however, these foods are not as healthy as the manufacturer claims. Some foods use several types of sugars and list them separately on the food label. Separated into smaller-sized groups, the sugars can be buried farther down on the ingredient list. Some gummy snacks claim "made with fruit" on their packages. The claim is technically true, but some might only have two grapes in each package. The rest is sugar. Even the labels on milk can be deceiving. Two percent milk claims to be low fat. However, most people do not know that milk is exempt from labeling laws that say a product has to have 3 grams of fat or less per serving to be called low fat. Two percent milk, however, has 5 grams of fat per serving. Three grams are saturated fats.

Changing Junk Food Behaviors

Many people find that changing their behavior is the most difficult part of breaking a junk food habit. But sometimes a few small steps can lead to long-lasting change. "If someone wants to cut down on junk food, they should replace one or two things at a time instead of cutting out everything at once,"[72] says Jack B., a teenager. Rudolph finds that changing their drink choices is one of the simplest moves for her new patients to make. "Maybe it's just cutting back on regular soda,"[73] she says.

Rudolph also counsels people to think about whether they are truly hungry when they open the refrigerator or reach for a snack. Many people snack on junk food because they have fallen into a behavior trap. Rudolph suggests asking, "Would I eat an apple?" If the answer is no, then the person is not truly hungry. If the answer is yes, try passing up

Healthy Snack Options

Instead of chips or cookies, the American Dietetic Association recommends several healthy snack options.

1. Peanut butter on apple slices.
2. Grated Monterey Jack cheese and salsa over a corn tortilla.
3. A banana dipped in yogurt and rolled in crushed cereal, and then frozen.
4. Celery sticks with peanut butter or low-fat cream cheese.
5. A mini pizza made with an English muffin, pizza sauce, and low-fat mozzarella cheese.
6. Homemade trail mix of cereal, raisins, and small pretzels.
7. Crunchy granola and blueberries on low-fat vanilla yogurt.
8. A snack kabob of alternating cubes of low-fat cheese and grapes on pretzel sticks.
9. A whole-grain waffle topped with low-fat yogurt and fruit.
10. Parmesan cheese on hot popcorn.

American Dietetic Association, "25 Healthy Snacks for Kids," Eatright.org. www.eatright.org/WorkArea/linkit.aspx?LinkIdentifier=id&ItemID=10825.

the junk food for a fruit or vegetable snack. To make access easy, try cutting up fruits and vegetables in advance and placing in easy-to-reach, clear containers. A person is more likely to choose a healthy choice if it is also an easy choice.

Meal Planning and Cooking

Many times people eat junk food because it is quick, easy, and convenient. With a little advance planning, healthy choices can be just as easy. At school, eating a sack lunch from home is a safe way to control food choices and portion sizes. At home, fill the shelves with healthy, portable snacks,

People often eat junk food because it is quick and convenient. Filling your refrigerator with portable foods like yogurt and vegetables can make it easy to snack healthily.

such as yogurt, cut-up fruits and vegetables, pretzels, popcorn, and mini whole wheat bagels.

Quick, planned meals can keep the temptation of fast food at bay. Plan meals for the week and make a grocery-shopping list. Make and freeze healthy dinners that can be defrosted quickly on busy nights. Another tip is to cook one night and reuse food in other recipes during the week. For example, leftovers from a roasted chicken can be added to salads, sandwiches, or homemade soup. People who plan ahead are less likely to reach for a convenient fast food meal.

Even if a food is healthy, it can be turned into junk food by frying or adding unhealthy ingredients or sauces. Instead of frying in oil, try baking, grilling broiling, steaming, or slow cooking foods. Herbs and spices can add flavor to food instead of high-fat condiments and sauces. "I think the best thing you can do is learn how to cook," says Elyse May, a teen who wrote her own cookbook. "That makes preparing and eating healthier foods more fun."[74]

Tips for Eating Out

Eating out does not have to be unhealthy. Once again, planning is important. People can ask waiters how food is prepared. Foods that are sautéed or have cream sauces are probably high in fat and calories. Lean, grilled menu items are usually better choices. Some restaurants even offer guides on their menu to show which items are low-fat, heart-healthy, or low-carbohydrate options.

Most fast food restaurants also serve low-fat, low-calorie options. They often have nutrition information available at the restaurant in order to compare menu items. Alternatively, many restaurants post nutrition information on corporate Web sites. At McDonald's a regular hamburger, side salad (without dressing), and apple dippers with caramel dip has only 375 calories and 10 grams of fat. At KFC an original-recipe chicken breast (without skin or breading), seasoned rice, and green beans has only 340 calories and 5.5 grams of fat.

Chantal's Success Story

Kicking a junk food habit takes hard work and commitment. For the past three years, sixteen-year-old Chantal Braziel has made healthy choices a part of her daily life. As a child Chantal was sedentary. She ate a lot of fried and junk food. At age twelve she visited the Weight Management and Wellness Center at the Children's Hospital of Pittsburgh. There she met with doctors and dieticians who told her that she was overweight and at risk of developing diabetes. After that first meeting she made a few changes to her diet, but Chantal admits that she was not fully committed. "It kind of wasn't a priority for me at that point. I knew I'd have to make changes in my life and that my glucose levels in my blood were high, but it took awhile for the commitment to kick in,"[75] she says.

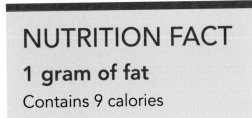

NUTRITION FACT

1 gram of fat
Contains 9 calories

About a year later Chantal noticed her weight increasing again. She decided to return to the clinic. "I could tell Chantal was ready to make those changes," says her mother.

"They told her once more everything she'd have to do to lose weight, and right away she began making the effort. She was older, more mature and she took responsibility for her life."[76]

This time Chantal stuck to the healthy eating plan recommended by the clinic's dieticians. She reduced junk food snacking and began exercising. Her family also decided to change their eating habits with her. Her mother adapted recipes to cook in a more healthy way. She also tries to keep fried food and sodas out of the house.

The hard work is paying off for Chantal. Her body fat has dropped from 41.3 percent to 27.4 percent. She wants to lose about 10 more pounds (4.5kg) and make sure her glucose levels stay within a healthy range. "It's been a long road for me and I had to grow up a little in order to keep motivating myself,"[77] says Chantal.

Aaron Snyder—Turning Back Diabetes

Aaron Snyder is the author of *The New Diabetes Prescription*. He describes how he was diagnosed with type 2 diabetes at a young age:

> I was 22 when I was officially diagnosed as a type II diabetic. I was a big time binge eater at the time. I would have candy bar raids, grab fast food, and go to Ben & Jerry's and eat two sundaes at a time. It didn't matter. I had a friend who was a type II diabetic who recognized my symptoms of thirst, excessive hunger, blurry vision, tingling fingers, and frequent urination. She checked my blood sugar after a large dinner and discovered it was around 211 mg/dl (the maximum normal level is 120 mg/dl). I confirmed the amateur diagnosis with a doctor's visit, which confirmed I was in fact very diabetic. At the time, I was around 50 to 60 pounds overweight.[78]

The diagnosis was a wake-up call for Snyder. He had multiple family members who suffered from complications of diabetes. "My great grandmother had multiple strokes, could not speak, and had a wooden leg when she died. My grandfather died blind of kidney failure in his early 50s. I did not want to end up like them,"[79] he says.

Healthy and Inexpensive

Many people complain that healthy food often costs more than junk or fast food. Here are five inexpensive foods that pack a powerful nutritional punch.

1. Apples: This easy-to-eat fruit is high in fiber, low in calories, and costs less than $1 per serving.
2. Bananas: This fruit is great to eat by itself or blended into smoothies or yogurts. A single serving costs about 45 cents.
3. Dry lentils: They are great for soups and stews. These little beans hold lots of protein and fiber. A two-ounce serving costs as little as 14 cents.
4. Oranges: In season, oranges are a great way to get fiber, vitamin C, and vitamin A. A single orange only costs about 40 cents.
5. Barley: Pearl barley is a healthy addition to soups, stews, salads, and casseroles. It adds fiber, protein, and iron to every meal. A two-ounce serving costs about 12 cents.

Snyder immediately went on a low-carbohydrate diet to get his blood sugar under control. He stopped eating junk food and started exercising. The diet and lifestyle changes had noticeable effects. "My blood sugar came down dramatically, I lost 60 pounds, my cholesterol and blood pressure improved, and I no longer needed the meds for diabetes prescribed to me,"[80] he says.

Today healthy food choices are a regular part of Snyder's day. He wrote about his experiences in *The New Diabetes Prescription*. He also reminds others that

it's not just one brownie, or one burger, or one milk shake. It's a habit, and you need to replace that habit with a different one. If you literally wrote down all the sugary cereal, candy, cookies, chips, pizza, cokes, burgers, and fries you ate in one week, and compared that to everything healthy you ate, you'd be shocked. Eating healthy is a way of life, and it happens from having delicious healthy food that you want to eat. You need to look forward to your meals and crave them as you once did unhealthy meals. When you know how to prepare healthy food that you enjoy, you'll then be a different person. That is the key.[81]

Try It at Home: Eating Healthier

Having ideas for food choices that are easy to cook and delicious to eat is a great way to avoid junk food cravings. They might even turn a junk food junkie into a healthy eater.

Breakfast Makeover

Breakfast is one of the most important meals of the day. Many people start the day by eating breakfast foods full of refined carbohydrates, such as white bagels, muffins, doughnuts, or sugary cereals. These foods have little protein or fiber. Most health experts recommend that a better way to fuel the body in the morning is to eat a breakfast full of complex carbohydrates and lean proteins. Whole grains, fruits, and vegetables contain complex carbohydrates. Low-fat or nonfat dairy, egg whites, egg substitutes, or lean breakfast meats are good sources of lean proteins. This type of breakfast will help people stay full until lunch and give them enough energy for their morning activities.

Nutrition experts at the Mayo Clinic recommend these quick, healthy breakfast choices.

- Cooked oatmeal with almonds or dried fruit
- Whole-wheat crackers with peanut butter or low-fat cheese
- Whole grain waffle spread with peanut butter
- Multigrain pancakes topped with fruit and low-fat yogurt

- A smoothie made with fruit, low-fat yogurt, and wheat germ
- A tortilla wrap filled with vegetables, salsa, and low-fat cheese

Breakfasts like oatmeal with fruit have complex carbohydrates that help a person stay full longer and avoid snacking.

Lunch Time Ideas

A lunch full of whole grains and low-fat proteins will help fuel a person past a mid-afternoon slump. Lunch is also a great time to add some servings of dairy and vegetables. The American Dietetic Association recommends several quick and tasty choices instead of waiting in the fast food line for a burger.

- A baked potato topped with broccoli, low-fat cheese, or salsa has fiber, calcium, and fewer calories than french fries.
- Sandwiches made of lean beef, ham, turkey, or chicken provide low-fat protein. Whole-grain breads and

vegetables add fiber and nutrients. Instead of mayonnaise or oil, these sandwiches can be spiced up with healthier condiments such as mustard, ketchup, salsa, or low-fat spreads.

- Salads made with dark leafy greens, carrots, peppers, and other vegetables are loaded with vitamins. Low-fat turkey or chicken on top adds protein to the meal.
- Sandwich wraps made from a soft tortilla and filled with rice, seafood or grilled chicken, and vegetables are a tasty low-fat lunch option. Avoiding high-fat dressings and spreads keeps a sandwich wrap a healthy choice.

Snack Time Changes

For many people, snack time is a junk food trap. The American Dietetic Association recommends several snacking tips.

- A person should snack only when he or she is hungry. Snacking when bored, frustrated, or stressed is never a good idea. Instead, activities, such as taking a walk, may relieve boredom or stress without snacking.
- Snacks should be portion-controlled. It is easier to control snacking when single-serving packages or portions are available.
- Good snacking is planned in advance. It is easy to keep a variety of nutritious, ready-to-eat snacks, such as baby carrots and low-fat dip or low-fat cheese and whole-grain crackers, on hand.

Make Dinner Healthy

There are many different ways to make a quick and tasty dinner without standing in the fast food line. The American Dietetic Association recommends these tips to make over the dinner meal.

- Instead of frying in butter or oil, a healthier way to prepare lean meats is to bake, broil, roast, stew, or stir-fry. This simple change will eliminate added fat and calories from the butter and oil.

Visual Guidelines for Serving Size

Portion control is an important part of healthy eating. Use these guidelines provided by the National Dairy Council to help estimate portion size.

Serving Size	Visual Guideline
A medium apple or peach is about the size of a tennis ball.	🍎🍑 = ⚪
1 ounce of cheese is about the size of 4 stacked dice.	🧀 = 🎲
1/2 cup of ice cream is about the size of a tennis ball.	🍨 = ⚪
1 cup of mashed potatoes or broccoli is about the size of your fist.	🥦 = ✊
1 teaspoon of butter or peanut butter is about the size of the tip of your thumb.	🧈 = 👍
1 ounce of nuts or small candies equals one handful.	✋ = 1 oz.

Taken from: Healthy Behaviors 4 Life, "Seven Ways to Size Up Servings," *Children's Hospital of Pittsburgh.*
http://hb4life.com/landing/learnAbout_Nutrition_sizeUpServings.html.

- Non-stick sprays and pans can substitute for butter and oils when cooking. This also eliminates added fat and calories.
- Dried beans and lentils added to homemade soup or chili provide extra protein and fiber. Vegetables, such as corn and tomatoes, can add extra vitamins to a soup, stew, or chili.
- Instead of salt, many foods can be seasoned with herbs, spices, garlic, onions, peppers, and lemon or lime juice. This reduces sodium in the meal.

Learning to stir-fry vegetables instead of frying them can help eliminate added fat and calories from butter.

- Heart-healthy fish is a great dinner option. Different ways of cooking fish, such as baking, broiling, grilling, and poaching, add variety.

Small Steps

Being a junk food junkie is not a life sentence. Armed with the knowledge to choose and prepare healthy foods, even the biggest junkies can change their eating habits. Taking small steps is a start in the right direction. Changing one snack or one meal at a time can eventually lead to a lifetime of healthy eating.

NOTES

Introduction: Junk Food Society

1. Quoted in Lesli Maxwell, "Ban Junk Food, Sodas in Schools, Prominent Scientists Recommend," *Education Week*, May 2, 2007, p. 7.

Chapter 1: The Popularity of Junk Food

2. Laurie Beebe, e-mail to the author, September 12, 2009.
3. Quoted in Craig Lambert, "The Way We Eat Now," *Harvard Magazine*, May–June 2004. http://harvard magazine.com/2004/05/the-way-we-eat-now.html.
4. Ellen Martin, interview with the author, September 12, 2009.
5. Beebe, e-mail.
6. Quoted in David A. Kessler, *The End of Overeating*. New York: Rodale, 2009, p. 13.
7. Quoted in Kessler, *The End of Overeating*, p. 13.
8. Quoted in *New Scientist*, "How Fatty Food Tickles the Tongue," November 5, 2005, p. 17.
9. Quoted in Kessler, *The End of Overeating*, p. 15.
10. Nancy Jerominski, e-mail to the author, September 18, 2009.
11. Morgan M., interview with the author, September 15, 2009.
12. Quoted in Anne Underwood, "That's Why We Call It Junk Food." *Newsweek*, December 8, 2003. HighBeam Research. http://www.highbeam.com/doc/1G1-110744041.html.
13. Quoted in Anne Underwood, "That's Why We Call It Junk Food."
14. Quoted in *Business Insurance*, "Medical Research on Diet, Stress Is Sweet News for Junk Food Fans," February 4, 2008, p. 23.
15. Morgan M., interview.
16. Quoted in Serena Gordon, "Gene May Make Kids Crave Junk Food," *Washington Post*, December 10, 2008. www.washingtonpost.com/wp-dyn/content/article/2008/12/10/AR2008121002713.html.

Chapter 2: How Junk Food Affects Your Health

17. Caiti, e-mail to the author, September 9, 2009.
18. Jerominski, e-mail.
19. Jerominski, e-mail.
20. Jack B., e-mail to author, September 10, 2009.
21. Quoted in *Dallas Morning News*, "California Study Links Soda to Obesity Epidemic," September 22,

2009. www.dallasnews.com/shared content/dws/fea/taste/stories/ DN-nh_sodahealth.ART.State. Edition1.4bd70e6.html.

22. Quoted in *New York Amsterdam News*, "Junk Food Is Unhealthy Recipe for Life," April 24, 2003, p. 18.

23. Quoted in Nancy Hellmich, "Childhood Obesity: A Lifetime of Danger," *USA Today*, January 14, 2008. www.usatoday.com/news/health/ weightloss/2008-01-13-childhood-obesity_N.htm.

24. Quoted in Mary Brophy Marcus, "Experts: Most Type 2 Diabetes Can Be Stopped in Childhood," *USA Today*, June 22, 2009. www .usatoday.com/news/health/2009-06-21-kids-diabetes_N.htm.

25. Quoted in Marcus, "Experts."

26. Quoted in Jenny Hope, "Junk Food Diet Linked to Cancer in Women," (London) *Daily Mail*, March 27, 2007. www.dailymail.co.uk/health/ article-443531/Junk-food-diet-linked-cancer-women.html.

27. Quoted in Hope, "Junk Food Diet Linked to Cancer in Women."

28. Quoted in Hope, "Junk Food Diet Linked to Cancer in Women."

29. Quoted in Rachel Dixon, "'Supersize Me' Mice Research Offers Grim Warning for America's Fast Food Consumers," Saint Louis University, May 24, 2007. www.slu.edu/ x15990.xml.

30. Quoted in Dixon, "'Supersize Me' Mice Research Offers Grim Warning for America's Fast Food Consumers."

31. Quoted in Children's Hospital Boston, "Quick-Burning Carbs May Cause Fatty Liver," Harvard Medical School, September 20, 2007. www.childrenshospital.org/news room/Site1339/mainpageS1339P 1sublevel341.html.

32. Quoted in Jeff Otto, "Interview: Morgan Spurlock," IGN Movies, May 4, 2004. http://movies.ign.com/ articles/511/511370p1.html.

33. Quoted in Contactmusic, "Morgan Spurlock Syndicated Interview." www.contactmusic.com/new/home .nsf/webpages/supersizemex02x 09x04.

34. Quoted in Contactmusic, "Morgan Spurlock Syndicated Interview."

35. Quoted in Contactmusic, "Morgan Spurlock Syndicated Interview."

36. Michelle May, e-mail to the author, September 14, 2009.

Chapter 3: Hooking the Youngest Eaters

37. Quoted in Serena Gordon, "Junk Food, TV Driving Kids to Obesity," *U.S. News & World Report*, September 25, 2007. http://health. usnews.com/usnews/health/health day/070925/junk-food-tv-driving-kids-to-obesity.htm.

38. Quoted in Kaiser Family Foundation, "The Role of Media in Childhood Obesity," February 2004. www .kff.org/entmedia/upload/The-Role-Of-Media-in-Childhood-Obesity.pdf.

39. Quoted in Kevin Freking, "Children's Ads Provide Junk Food for

Thought," *The Mercury*, October 6, 2008. www.commercialfreechild hood.org/news/2008/10/junkfood thought.htm.

40. Quoted in Catherine Holahan, "Crying Foul over Online Junk Food Marketing," *Bloomberg Businessweek*, August 12, 2008. www.businessweek.com/tech nology/content/aug2008/tc2008 0811_394016.htm.

41. Quoted in Kate Devlin, "Celebrities Like Cheryl Cole and David Beckham 'Should Not Endorse Junk Food,'" *Daily Telegraph* (London), March 20, 2009. www.telegraph .co.uk/health/healthnews/5023647/ Celebrities-like-Cheryl-Cole-and-David-Beckham-should-not-endorse-junk-food.html.

42. Quoted in Holahan, "Crying Foul over Online Junk Food Marketing."

43. Quoted in Australian Communications and Media Authority, "ACMA Media Release 118/2009—1 September," Commonwealth of Australia, September 1, 2009. www.acma .gov.au/WEB/STANDARD..PC/ pc=PC_311872.

44. Quoted in School Nutrition Association, "School Nutrition Association Releases 'State of School Nutrition 2009' Survey," August 4, 2009. www.schoolnutrition.org/Blog. aspx?id=12832&blogid=564.

45. Quoted in Adam Bornstein, "Why Are Schools Selling Junk Food to Kids?" *Men's Health*, November 2008. http://www.menshealth.com/ men/nutrition/food-for-fitness/ nutrition-junk-food-and-kids/article/ 24949179b69c110vgnvcm100000 13281eac.

46. Quoted in Bornstein, "Why Are Schools Selling Junk Food to Kids?"

47. Quoted in Bornstein, "Why Are Schools Selling Junk Food to Kids?"

48. Quoted in Lloyd de Vries, "Deal Curbs Soda Sales in Schools," CBS News, May 3, 2006. www.cbsnews .com/stories/2006/05/03/health/ main1575707.shtml.

49. Quoted in Annys Shin, "Removing Schools' Soda Is Sticky Point," *Washington Post*, March 22, 2007. www. washingtonpost.com/wp-dyn/ content/article/2007/03/21/AR 2007032101966.html.

50. Quoted in Maxwell, "Ban Junk Food, Sodas in Schools, Prominent Scientists Recommend," p. 7.

Chapter 4: Taking Responsibility

51. Quoted in *Archives of Pediatrics & Adolescent Medicine*, "Kids Mimic Parents' Diets from an Early Age," Reuters, November 3, 2008. www .reuters.com/article/healthNews/ idUSTRE4A26J920081103.

52. Quoted in MedicineNet, "Junk Food vs. Healthy Nutrition for Children." www.medicinenet.com/script/ main/art.asp?articlekey=9522.

53. Duncan Fine, "Junk Food Doesn't Make Kids Fat—Junk Parents Do," *Punch*, September 2009. www

.thepunch.com.au/articles/junk-food-doesnt-make-kids-fat-junk-parents-do.

54. Beebe, e-mail.

55. Elyse May, e-mail to the author, September 14, 2009.

56. Quoted in Michael Park, "Lawyers See Fat Payoffs in Junk Food Lawsuits," Fox News, January 23, 2002. www.foxnews.com/story/0,2933,43735,00.html.

57. Quoted in Jonathan Wald, "McDonald's Obesity Suit Tossed," CNN Money, February 17, 2003. http://money.cnn.com/2003/01/22/news/companies/mcdonalds.

58. United States District Court, Southern District of New York, *Pelman and Bradley v. McDonald's,* January 22, 2003, p. 43. www.casewatch.org/civil/mcdonalds/dismissal.pdf.

59. Quoted in Ted Barrett, "House Bans Fast-Food Lawsuits," CNN, March 10, 2004. www.cnn.com/2004/LAW/03/10/fat.lawsuits/index.html.

60. Quoted in Jennifer Ordoñez, "Taking the Junk out of Junk Food," *Newsweek*, October 8, 2007. www.newsweek.com/id/41875.

61. Quoted in Ordoñez, "Taking the Junk out of Junk Food."

62. Quoted in Michelle Conlin and John Cady, "Hide the Doritos! Here Comes HR," *Bloomberg Businessweek*, April 17, 2008. www.businessweek.com/magazine/content/08_17/b4081094075494.htm?chan=magazine+channel_what percent27s+next.

63. Quoted in Patricia Odell, "Coke, Pepsi Vow to Eliminate Worldwide Marketing to Kids Under 12," *Promo Magazine*, May 21, 2008. http://commercialfreechildhood.org/news/cokepepsi.htm.

64. Quoted in Odell, "Coke, Pepsi Vow to Eliminate Worldwide Marketing to Kids Under 12."

65. Quoted in Graeme Hamilton, "The Junk Food Wars," *National Post*, January 27, 2009. www.commercialfreechildhood.org/news/2009/01/junkfoodwars.html.

66. Quoted in MSNBC, "New York City Passes Trans Fat Ban," December 5, 2006. www.msnbc.msn.com/id/16051436.

67. Quoted in Jennifer Steinhauer, "California Bans Restaurant Use of Trans Fats," *New York Times*, July 26, 2008. www.nytimes.com/2008/07/26/us/26fats.html?_r=2.

68. Quoted in Maggie Fox, "Tax Junk Food, Drinks to Fight Child Obesity Report," Reuters, September 1, 2009. www.reuters.com/article/latestCrisis/idUSN31395859.

69. Quoted in Karen Kaplan, "Junkfood Tax Idea Is Gaining Weight," *Los Angeles Times*, August 23, 2009. www.latimes.com/news/nationworld/nation/la-sci-junk-food-tax23-2009aug23,0,5244082.story.

70. Quoted in Lisa Baertlein and Maggie Fox, "Battle Lines Drawn over Soda, Junk Food Taxes," Reuters, September 1, 2009. www.reuters.com/article/healthNews/idUSTRE5806E520090901?pageNumber=2&virtualBrandChannel=11604&sp=true.

Chapter 5: Are You a Junk Food Junkie?

71. Kristen Rudolph, interview with the author, October 8, 2009.
72. Jack B., e-mail.
73. Rudolph, interview.
74. May, e-mail.
75. Quoted in Healthy Behaviors 4 Life, "Chantal's Story," Children's Hospital of Pittsburgh. http://hb4life.com/landing/successStories_chantal.html.
76. Quoted in Healthy Behaviors 4 Life, "Chantal's Story."
77. Quoted in Healthy Behaviors 4 Life, "Chantal's Story."
78. Aaron Snyder, e-mail to the author, October 8, 2009.
79. Snyder, e-mail.
80. Snyder, e-mail.
81. Snyder, e-mail.

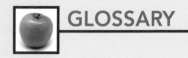

body mass index (BMI): A calculation that uses a person's height and weight to estimate how much body fat he or she has.

chronic: Occurring for a long time.

competitive foods: Foods sold in schools outside the official school lunch program. They can include foods and drinks in vending machines, school stores, and á la carte lunch stations.

epidemic: A rapid spread or the increase in occurrence of something, such as a disease.

glycemic: Having glucose in the blood.

nutrients: Substances in food, such as vitamins and minerals, that are necessary for growth and life.

obese: Extremely fat or overweight. An adult with a body mass index (BMI) of 30 or higher is considered obese.

palatable: Agreeable, as tastes or smells.

satiate: To satisfy to fullness.

sleep apnea: A temporary suspension of breathing that occurs during sleep.

triglycerides: The chemical form in which most fat exists in the body and blood.

ORGANIZATIONS TO CONTACT

American Dietetic Association (ADA)

120 S. Riverside Plaza, Suite 2000
Chicago, IL 60606-6995
phone: (800) 877-1600
Web site: www.eatright.org

The ADA is the world's largest organization of food and nutrition professionals. The ADA Web site features timely, science-based food and nutrition information.

Campaign for a Commercial-Free Childhood (CCFC)

Judge Baker Children's Center
53 Parker Hill Ave.
Boston, MA 02120
phone: (617) 278-4172
fax: (617) 232-7343
e-mail: ccfc@jbcc.harvard.edu
Web site: www.commercialexploitation.org

The CCFC is a national coalition of health-care professionals, educators, advocacy groups, parents, and individuals devoted to limiting the impact of the commercial culture on children. The CCFC Web site provides information about the debate over junk food marketing and advertising to children.

Center for Science in the Public Interest

1875 Connecticut Ave. NW, Suite 300
Washington, DC 20009
phone: (202) 332-9110
fax: (202) 265-4954
Web site: www.cspinet.org

The Center for Science in the Public Interest is an advocate for nutrition and health, food safety, alcohol policy, and sound science. It circulates a newsletter, and its Web site offers many resources to learn about the latest news and science related to junk food and nutrition.

USDA Center for Nutrition Policy and Promotion

3101 Park Center Dr., Room 1034
Alexandria, VA 22302-1594
phone: (888) 779-7264
Web site: www.mypyramid.gov

The Center for Nutrition Policy and Promotion is part of the U.S. Department of Agriculture. Its goal is to improve the nutrition and well-being of Americans. The center's staff of nutritionists and dietitians can answer basic food and nutrition questions.

World Health Organization (WHO)

Avenue Appia 20
1211 Geneva 27
Switzerland
phone: + 41 22 791 21 11
fax: + 41 22 791 31 11
Web site: www.who.int/en

WHO is the arm of the United Nations that is responsible for providing leadership and guidance on global health matters. WHO addresses world nutrition as one of its health topics and devotes a section of its Web site to nutrition issues.

FOR MORE INFORMATION

Books

Stephen Currie, *Junk Food*. Ann Arbor, MI: Cherry Lake, 2009. This book provides a short overview of what junk food is, how it affects health, and how to eat better.

Eric Schlosser and Charles Wilson, *Chew on This*. Boston: Houghton Mifflin, 2006. This book gives a behind-the-scenes look at the fast food industry, written by the author of the best-selling adult title *Fast Food Nation*.

Ellen Shanley and Colleen Thompson, *Fueling the Teen Machine*. Boulder, CO: Bull, 2001. This title presents teens with the latest information on a wide range of food topics, including nutrition, junk food, eating disorders, and vegetarianism. It also gives teens tips for cooking.

DVD

Super Size Me. Directed by Morgan Spurlock. Culver City, CA: Sony Pictures, 2003. In this PG-13 documentary about the commercial food industry, filmmaker Morgan Spurlock makes himself a test subject. After eating a diet of McDonald's fast food three times a day for a month straight, Spurlock shows the physical and mental effects of consuming fast food.

Internet Source

Craig Lambert, "The Way We Eat Now," *Harvard Magazine*, May–June 2004. http://harvardmagazine.com/2004/05/the-way-we-eat-now.html.

Web Sites

Food Network (www.foodnetwork.com/healthy-eating). The healthy eating section of the Food Network Web site features recipes for low-fat cooking, whole grains, favorite recipe makeovers, and vegetarian and healthy snacks.

KidsHealth (www.kidshealth.org). This Web site offers kids and teens sections that have information about healthy eating and nutrition. Learn about food labels, fats, proteins, and carbohydrates. The site also offers healthy recipes to try.

MyPyramid.gov, United States Department of Agriculture (www

.mypyramid.gov). This Web site offers interactive tools, menu planners, podcasts, and information about healthy eating.

Nutrition.com (www.nutrition.com .sg/ho). Nutrition.com offers pages for children and teens with information about healthy eating. There is nutrition information on several fast food restaurants. Teens can also try the nutrition calculators to figure out their body mass index, waist-to-hip ratio, and estimated daily calorie needs.

INDEX

A

Advertising/marketing, 15–16
  banning, 49–51
  children/teens as targets of, 42–48
  role of government in regulating, 69–70
  spending by food industry on, 62
American Idol (TV program), 68
American Public Health Association, 58
Arteries
  hypertension and, 32
  plaque build up in, 30, *31*
Athletes, 28

B

Beckham, David, 48, *49*
Body mass index (BMI), 27
  increase in average, 12
Brain, 20–21
Braziel, Chantal, 81–82

C

Calcium, 37
Cancer
  junk food associated with, 34–35
  link to obesity, 30
Carbohydrates
  blood sugar levels and, 25–26
  liver/gall bladder disease and, 36–37
  means of conversion into energy, 35
  refined, 84
  simple *vs.* complex, 24

Cartoons
  promoting fruits/vegetables, 45
  promoting junk food, 45–46
Centers for Disease Control and
  Prevention (CDC), 72
Children/adolescents
  dietary needs of fat/sugar, 9
  fast food addiction in, 22
  marketing to, 42–48
  obesity among, 27–28, 30
  tend to choose junk food at school,
    52–53
Cholecystokinin (CCK), 22, *22*
Cholesterol, 30
  HDL, 65
  LDL, 31, 64
Cloudy With A Chance Of Meatballs
  (film), 46–47
Coca-Cola
  agrees to limit marketing to children,
    49, 68
  expansion into South America, 14
  Internet marketing by, 48
  school contracts with, 55
Cravings, 19–20

D

Department of Agriculture, U.S. (USDA),
  52
Diabetes. *See* Type 2 diabetes
Diseases, 30
  See also specific diseases

avoiding *vs.* limiting, 40–41
cancer and, 34–35
cardiovascular disease and, 31–32
as comfort food, 21
definition of, 9–10
employers taking action against,
    66–68
genetics and attraction to, 23
health problems associated with, 7–8
immigrants struggle with, 18
liver/gall bladder disease and, 35–37
popularity of, 6–7
processing/flavoring of, 19
reasons for choosing, 13, 15
taxing of, 71–73
type 2 diabetes and, 32, 34
See also Fast food

K

Kaiser Family Foundation, 72

L

Liver/liver disease, *35*, 35–36

M

May, Elyse, 61, 80
McDonald's, *14*, 38, 40, 49
    amount of exercise and, *63*
    cross-promotions and, 46–47
    Internet marketing by, 47–48
    lawsuit against, 62–64
    low fat/low calories options at, 81
    obesity crisis among Okinawans
        and, 33

N

National School Lunch Program (U.S.
    Department of Agriculture), 51–52

New England Journal of Medicine, 23
The New Diabetes Prescription (Snyder),
    82, 83–84

O

Obesity, 8
    among Okinawans, 33
    cost of, 58
    health effects of, 30
    prevalence in U.S., 27
    rise in, 12
    soda as major contributor to, 29
Opinion polls. *See* Surveys

P

Pancreas, 32, 35
Parents
    role in promoting healthy eating
        habits, 57, 59–61
    toddlers allowed junk food by, 42
Partnership for Prevention, 58
PBS (Public Broadcasting Service), 45
PepsiCo, *49*, 68
    school contracts with, 54–55
    use of celebrity endorsements, 48
Polls. *See* Surveys
Processed food, 12

R

Rudolph, Kristen, 75, 76, 78

S

Salt
    taste of food and, 16, 17–18
    ways of reducing in diet, 87
Salty foods
    cravings for, 20
    hypertension and, 31–32
School Nutrition Association, 52

PICTURE CREDITS

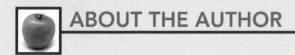

Carla Mooney received her undergraduate degree in economics from the University of Pennsylvania. She has written several books for young people, including *Bioethics* and *Online Social Networking*. Mooney lives with her husband and three children in Pittsburgh, Pennsylvania.